Spanish Mustangs

and

Hard Times

Mabel "Dipper" Brislawn
Recounts
Sunshine and Rain
*

Robert E. Brislawn Sr.'s
Unceasing
Defense of the Spanish Mustang.

i

Spanish Mustangs

and

Hard Times

Mabel "Dipper" Brislawn

Bob Brislawn Memorial Society

Publisher

First Printing: <2014>

ISBN-13:
978-1500552930

Table of Contents

ix

x

Overview

by Dipper Brislawn

Unexpected Danger Strikes the Horses of the West

Our friend, the Eminent Lawrence P. Richards, Ph.D of Zoology, who was among the founders of the Spanish Mustang Registry, Incorporated, told me that it is generally believed horses actually evolved in North America, as fossils of horses are found here. These early horses on the South and North American continents were all gone by the time Columbus arrived. But they don't know how long ago nor why they all died; perhaps it was some mysterious illness like sleeping sickness. So horses had to be imported and raised for the conquest of both South and North America.

These horses, imported or raised, were the old time Spanish ponies used by the Conquistadores, the earliest explorers. Horses gone wild or stolen from the  Spaniards were the source for the Indians who were mounted on Spanish horses by the 1700's. The fur trappers and mountain men traded with the Indians for Spanish horses. The Pony express riders rode Spanish ponies as well as the cowboy who brought the longhorns up the trail from Texas. They were used by homesteaders and cattlemen in all areas of the New World, were driven and ridden by gentlemen, scholars and ladies, were used to pull stagecoaches, the wagons on cattle roundups and ore cars in the mines. It was the Spanish Horses who pulled the plows and the Fresnos for the dirt work when the roads and railroads were built as well as the irrigation canals that carried the water that made the desert bloom that raised the food for us all. They carried the mail in all types of weather and out ran the robbers/highwaymen. Also they faced dangers of mountain lions, blizzards and drought, and they flourished. They were the Horse of the West. But they faced an unexpected danger.

During the United States Government's campaign to conquer the Indians, the plan was to subdue the Indians and put them on reservations by killing off all the buffalo. They eliminated the Indian's food supply, hides for clothing and their teepees, by shooting the buffalo, by paying a bounty on each buffalo tongue the glory hunters brought in. I read that it took only 20 years to kill all the buffalo. A very few remained, maybe six left in Oklahoma, when someone gathered them up to preserve and save them from extinction.

At the same time that the United States Government was glorifying people for the wanton slaughter of buffalo, they were promoting people to destroy the Indian's horses, as well, to exterminate their means of transportation. This policy carried over even after the Indians were on reservations.

For instance: In 1877 when General Oliver O. Howard and General Nelson A. Miles chased Chief Joseph and the men, women and children of the Nez Perce Tribe, to capture and put them on a reservation. Chief Joseph and his Tribe in their attempt to escape into Canada were in flight for eleven weeks. With Spanish ponies they covered sixteen hundred miles across the rugged mountains of

2

Idaho, Wyoming and Montana. They engaged ten separate United States military commands in thirteen battles and skirmishes, and in most cases defeated the army or fought them to a standstill. They were thirty miles from the Canadian Border when due to the cold and severe conditions Chief Joseph surrendered on October 5, 1877. The Nez Perce gave up eleven hundred horses and one hundred saddles and were forced to walk hundreds of miles to a reservation. (This information is from Indian Oratory by W. C. Vanderwerth. Describing this campaign, General William T. Sherman said it was "one of the most extraordinary wars of which there is any record.")

I have read in other sources that those horses, taken from Chief Joseph and his tribe, were all shot to death; and the people made to walk back.

General Custer killed 800 Indian ponies at one of his attacks on an Indian Village. How many were killed at Custer's other attacks on other Indian Villages?

On the Crow Reservation 40,000 horses were killed by the government. A bounty of $4.00 was paid for ears. Another idea and policy of the Government was to introduce new stallions into the Indian's herds and by cross breeding eliminate the breed. However, the Indians would often eat the new stallions, thereby sometimes foiling the government's plan.

This extermination carried over even to the mixed blood wild range horses because people couldn't distinguish between a horse of mixed bloodlines and the true Spanish Horses of long ago.

As a result of these actions, the original horse of the West was almost gone by the early 1900's.

This was the situation that existed in 1911 when a young man named Bob Brislawn began packing for the U. S. Geological Survey.

Before photogrammetric surveying techniques, surveyors had to gain access to every peak and canyon. Horses were used to do this. Bob discovered that many of the horses being used in the Survey's pack string were Indian ponies - pure Spanish Mustangs. He also discovered that they were the best. They were small, agile, hardy. Their narrow chests and short backs allowed them to navigate twisted mountain trails. They were intelligent, a faithful companion in camp or on the trail. These horses hung around camp, as wherever camp was they were home. If anything scared them they ran for you or camp for safety. They could exist on merely the meadow grasses and whatever other forage was available in the remote country without needing rations of grain.

Bob thought, no wonder the Indians could outrun the cavalry! No wonder they could loaf along, shoot a buffalo now and then, and still stay ahead! This horse must not be allowed to disappear.

According to J. Frank Dobie: "These horses bore Spanish explorers across two continents. They brought to the Plains Indians the age of horse culture. Texas cowboys rode them to extend the ranching occupation clear to the plains of Alberta. Spanish horse, Texas cow pony and mustang were all one in those times when, as sayings went, a man was no better than his horse and a man on foot was no man at all. Like the Longhorn, the mustang has been virtually bred out of existence. But mustang horses will always symbolize western frontiers, long trails of Longhorn herds, seas of pristine grass, and men riding free."

One Opinion:

To Continue to Eliminate the Old Horses
and Create a New Horse

The Taylor Grazing Act of 1934 under the Department of Agriculture, provided for the lease of some public lands for grazing. This Taylor Grazing Act ended the unregulated grazing of public grazing lands; they controlled the Public Domain. What is now called the Bureau of Land Management was established in 1946. Wild Horse Runners were allowed to round up the horses for slaughter.

The Taylor Grazing Act's policy was to shoot the horses and clear the land. They were supposedly preserving Wildlife, but they didn't consider horses as wildlife because they could not be shot and eaten by the game hunters.

The cow and sheep ranchers who were leasing the public land also shot the horses on sight because the horses ate grass a cow or sheep could eat.

When the people began the Quarter Horse Registry they started out with a plan to **create** a horse to replace the old time Western horse and to have only one type of horse. By using the Spanish horse as their foundation stock's bloodlines, they have developed a wonderful all around using horse. The big buck money boys were behind them. As well as creating a new horse, the old should be preserved for posterity. The equine species should retain its genetic diversity.

The Other Opinion Was to Save the Horses

Bob had put in thirty seasons with the United States Geological Survey--Topagraghic Branch. when they still used these Spanish horses. But he found these Spanish horses were becoming harder and harder to find. Bob knew there were very few left as he provided these horses for most of those surveys over those thirty years. as well as being horse wrangler and packer. He knew the horses from on the ground experience and when he was young, knowledge that old-timers could teach him that went back 100 years. There was lots of talk and concern by our friends and relatives, that soon these horses would become extinct. These people didn't know of any Spanish horses left. However, nothing was being done.

There were two men in particular who told Bob that he was the one to save the horses. John Blackburn, his Survey boss, told Bob to gather and save the Indian/Spanish horses. Horses like Ping and Pong. (the ones they used on the Survey 1911 thru 1920's). The other, a survey co-worker, Jim Clark of Boseman, Montana, convinced him that HE would have to be one to do it.

Since "You have the knowledge of the horses and the land to run them on".

They were right.

However, Bob didn't have the breeding stock. He had a few old geldings that he used on the survey and on his ranch, but he needed mares and stallions. So began The Search.

To Save the Horses We Faced Ridicule and Laughter.

We went though Perdition and back out the other side, twice, for these horses. as my sister-in-law, Gioja says about me.

At that time many prominent (horse) people did not know nor believe the history of the Spanish horses. We had to PROVE it.

Then the latter day registries just took our `thunder' and scientific proof and built on it.

The people who set out to destroy the Spanish Mustang came to look for the Brislawn horse herd, the remnants Bob had gathered up, so those horses, too, could be sold through the sale rings to the killer market buyers.

More than one man came with big bucks $$$$'s to buy us out, lock, stock, and barrel, the whole horse herd, the land... whatever it took - but "NO" there, too. The world needs more men and women who can't be bought.

Bob saved these horses from extinction without help from the government nor anyone with the big money grants. None was asked for. In fact, some people would have paid the Big Buck Money NOT to save them. Or at least to bring them back in an impure state or type.

The Search for the Pure

Bob talked to everyone in our area and asked if they knew of any Mustangs left in the vastness of North America. Abe French, a friend and an old time horseman who rode for the Parks Lands and Cattle Company, Lightening Flats, Crook County, Wyoming, and who knew the pure Spanish horses told Bob there was a old mare on Lightening Flats. Bob and his eleven year old son, Emmett, rode the thirty miles up there to search for that old white Indian mare, It was a big area so on the first two trips they did not succeed. It was cold and rainy on their third trip up there when they found her, but the old mare already lay dying.

From Charley Williams, another neighbor, Bob learned about the Crow Indian horse herd Charley and his brother, Dick, trailed down to Moorcroft, Wyoming from Wyola, Montana and the Crow Reservation in 1925. There were still remnants of these horses and their colts left in our area. The horse colts had all been gelded and the fillies sold. Charley Williams still had a sorrel mare, Kate, who Bob bought. Charley Reynolds had a Williams mare, Penny. When Bob bought her, I rode her the eight miles home. Bill Grover had a William's mare, Queenie. Emmett rode her the six miles home. Now, we had the mares. But, we needed stallions.

When along in the fall of 1945 Monty and Sadie Holbrook and family, as Bob and Mary, were with them then, came by trading horses. The Holbrooks were mustang runners, who captured wild mustangs in the wilderness and rough canyons of Colorado, Utah and Wyoming. After capturing a sufficient number they trailed 1200 miles to Williston, North Dakota and then into Canada, trading or selling these horses on their way. They made six or seven trips over the years.

When the Holbrooks made their return trip south, in the fall of 1945, they happened to camp with their horses over night on the Cayuse

8

Ranch, in a small pasture by Bob's big reservoir along the D Road.

Bob bought two of their young stallions, Buckshot and Ute. but we needed more mares and stallions to keep the herds growing pure, so the search continued.

Somewhere in the vastness of the North American continent we knew there had to remain other remnants of the pure. Or was there? If so, where? In remote deserts and mountains? In canyons? In Indian herds free of draft and Eastern horses? In the herds of Indians' who had eaten the Government Thoroughbred stallions put in to "breed-up" the Indian pony? Maybe. We didn't know exactly where, but we knew somewhere they had to be.

So we searched. And others learned of our quest. Interest was growing.

Bob knew people all over the West, so wrote letters asking about the Spanish horses. Also, by word of mouth, people learned of Bob's search. We received letters from all over the country, asking us to come see their horses. many people believed that they had just what we were looking for. When we answered these letters we asked of their horse's history and of their ancestors.

Thereby, we narrowed down the areas that there could be pure blood left. We wrote articles in various western horse magazines to create interest and asked for any information that people had.

Bob wrote to the Indian Reservations and to big horse registries. After hearing about someone having what they thought was a Spanish Horse we would load up our camp gear in the old Terra-plane car, and set off driving to see what they had. As we could not leave the ranch work for a very long time, these trips were usually a one day drive; two or three days at the most.

We could tell at a glance that the horse in question was not what we were looking for. But to prove to the owners what we were talking about, Bob had a measuring stick, a 3 X 1 board with the measurements all marked off. At the height of 14 hands (if a hand be 4 inches), Bob had drilled a hole, and through that hole he had a twelve inch bolt that he held in place as the board was held against the horse's withers. Bob would not take a horse that was over 14.2 hands. Also the distance between the poll to the withers and the withers to the rump had to be equal. The Indians would lead out their horse and Bob would go get his stick to measure so it ended up when they led out another horse, they would say, "GET THE STICK". The Indians named him "Get the Stick" on all the reservations we visited.

Bob had his ranch work to do, besides being a father to his motherless children, so he was a busy man. We children had to help with the ranching, haying, feeding the cows and horses, and calving, besides attending the one room country school. We had cooking and housework at home, so our days too, were filled to the brim.

Therefore our research on the history and literature of the Spanish Horse and letter writing was done at night. At that time our only light was from a coal-oil lamp. We literally burned the midnight oil! We felt we were really advanced when Bob, our Dad, installed a 32-volt wind charger for electric lights.

We received huge piles of inquiry letters from people all over the world eager for information and pictures of the Spanish Horses.

After our trips to look at horses, we would return home to do the daily ranch work, and to answer those letters of inquiry. We would try to answer 15 a day, or 450 to 475 a month. We had a single mimeographed sheet as a form letter that helped, but we still had to answer other questions they may have asked so still needed to write it out in longhand.

Then was the time to study the historical material some more. We studied any and all history books, especially books by known horsemen. This was done while we saved up enough money for another trip to the remote areas of North America. Then go and do the ground work of contacting people, measuring the horses, listening to their horses' history, checking coat hairs and hair colors, the ears size and shape and the tufts of hair in each ear and the color there. He studied the distance or width between the eyes and how the eyes were placed on the side of the head. The eyes often had patches of white mixed in with the brown. Then looking at their horses' bones - going to fields and hills and digging through rotten carcasses, to seeing and measuring the bones, and vertebrae of the ancestors of their horses. We found that the horses vertebrae were different. As well as the coat hairs on the horses body and especially the ears. So many characteristics were different.

Later in 1956, Bob leased the Cayuse Ranch to his son, Emmett, so he could be free to travel in his search. Bob moved to Tijeras, New Mexico and we searched in every direction each weekend for two day camp-outs. We could not go very far away from home because the younger children, Colleen and Shane, were still going to school. Nejl was in the Army at this time.

There also, in Tijeras, we answered the mail, inquiries for any information, from school children to the leading horse registries, to western writers, and artists. Here I began t write down some of Bob's stories about the horses and the people who rode them.

The search and us then came home to the Cayuse Ranch, Oshoto, Wyoming to start the cycle all over again, continued year after year after year for seventeen years. May 1957, home to the Cayuse Ranch, Oshoto, Wyoming. There the first meeting of the Spanish Mustang Registry was held in June.

Then on June 14, 1957 we drove to the law office of Richard Macy, Attorney-at-law, in Sundance, Crook County, Wyoming. There the By-laws and Articles of Incorporation were signed forming The Spanish Mustang Registry, Incorporated. This was the very first registry of its kind. (Bob and I had wrote up the By-laws for the Spanish Mustang Registry before this and took them in for Attorney Richard Macy to put them into the legal words and terms so they were ready to be signed by the newly elected officials when we went in that day.)

We did it all without financial aid, without grants from big corporations, foundations, or government.

July 1957 I leased the Cayuse Ranch from Bob Brislawn, and tried to hold things together, while working for Richard (Dick) Macy, an Attorney at Law, Sundance, Wyoming. My brother, Shane, stayed with me in Sundance so he could attend high school. My sister, Colleen, also stayed with me part of the time, when not helping Bob on the Cayuse Ranch. Emmett wanted to go ride for the big ranches in the great Southwest and he did go. This time he went to Utah and then to Nevada where he worked for a big cattle outfit and rode with the wagon...and used pack horses out in the far country.

My Dad, Bob Brislawn, and my sister, Colleen stayed on the Cayuse Ranch. But, Bob was free to go and come with the research and traveling required with the Spanish Mustang Registry, Inc.

The Research and Search Continued On

In July of 1970, There was still a lot of interest in these horses. Twenty-seven years ago, at this writing, the Newsletter for the Spanish Mustang Registry reported that the secretary answered 400 letters during that month. Paul Hennessay, a teacher at the Brislawn School during the 1960's, said he remembers that Bob was always studying the bones of his own horse herd. Whenever one of the horses died, Bob would go out and look at it's backbone to check on how many vertebrae and ribs it had. He also took a look at the front legs for the round cannon bones. Then Bob would come in the house with his arms swinging and a huge smile on his face, saying that he was happy as to the pureness of the Spanish blood. The horse's bloodlines were alright. The bones proved him right. Not only did Bob study the vertebra's but the whole skeleton.

During the 1940's when Bob was searching for the remnants of the pure Spanish Mustangs. We were using horses in all the various aspects of the ranch work. With a team and wagon we hauled logs for the buildings, the corral poles and fence posts from the timber ten miles away. We used horse-drawn mowers,  rakes, sweeps, stackers, and haywagons, and during the winter we put the hayrack on the horse-drawn sled to haul out hay to feed the cows. Our closest neighbors were from three to thirteen miles so we either walked or rode over there to play with the children.

Everyone still used horses to go to town for groceries. The closest store was at Oshoto, with a population of eleven, which was seven miles away. We would ride the same saddle-horses or drive the same team of horses to attend church on Sundays, as church services were held in our own or neighbors homes. The priest would come ninety miles once a month from Newcastle, Wyoming.

Bob did have a car, but during the winters he jacked it up and put it on blocks, as he took off the tires/wheels and kept them and the car battery in the cellar all winter.

We were using horses in our everyday work, as well as digging through the rotten carcass of dozens of dead horses to see their backbone (Vertebra), take their head measurements and see their teeth. At times we even used `The Stick' to measure the carcass of the horses.

Besides all that I cooked the meals for the many visitors and cared for the family while writing letters for the research and answering the inquiries. The people and letters of inquiry came from all over the world.

During this time I was taming and training horses for Bob, Uncle Ferdie and others. Many times I received food as payment for some of the work I did when housecleaning or babysitting.

Any money I may have earned went to Bob for the trips in search of the old time Spanish pony.

I don't know why people ridiculed us, but we faced ridicule and laughter upon laughter but we never stopped or quit our search and research, as we knew better than those other people did. We were "dyed-in-the-wool" in our beliefs. The search continued even after the Spanish Mustang Registry, Incorporated, was founded, and the research continues even to this day.

The Spanish Mustangs are saved thanks to Bob Brislawn, but not to Bob, alone, as he had the following of a lot of dedicated horse lovers the world over. Like all great life-works there had to be others

14

who believed in him and his work who would carry on after he was dead. This is being done by Bob's family and the Registry that he founded.

I was Bob's secretary through all this; I helped with the mail, research, and then registrations of the horses. I also provided funds, any money I had went to this search. In the beginning I trained and schooled horses when the going price was 25.00 per head, and anything earned went into the research and ranch. With the Spanish Language course I took in high school, I could read the old Spanish journals and ship's logs and diaries of the people who were there, those who came over with Columbus, Cortez, DeSota and others, from the 1492/1500's and onwards. I had ordered and bought a huge book from South America that was written in Spanish which told of the types of Spanish horses there and records of the arrival of the horses to the Americas.

In this book also it showed the Skeletons and bone structures of their horses. From this book Bob got the idea that there was something different about the bones and vertebrae, and that was what we needed to prove the authenticity of the Spanish horses.

I do not remember the name of this book and at this time no one knows where the book is at.

Bob said, He couldn't have done it without me. but he had a lot of help from all of his five children and others who were interested in saving the Spanish Horses.

As Bob and I toiled over letters at night and with the horses and people in the day, Bob would often quote Longfellow's poem:

The heights by great men reached and kept; were not

attained by sudden flight.

But they, while their companions slept,

were toiling upwards in the night."

When driving to far places in search of Spanish Mustangs Bob would sometimes quote part of Robert Frost's poem:

"The Woods are lovely, dark and deep.

But I have promises to Keep,

and miles to go before I sleep,

and miles to go before I sleep."

Another Word from Dipper

 In 1963, Bob, while living near Finley, Oklahoma, wrote many stories of his life at the urging of his son, Nejl. Bob had written only about the horses until Nejl asked him to write the stories of his life as well. Nejl believed he could get them published. In 1964, Bob moved home to his Homestead Shack, Cayuse Ranch, near Oshoto, Wyoming where he continued to study, write, research, travel and promote the Spanish Horses -- the horse of the Indians, cowboys and mountain-men -- the horse who built the New World – America.

Bob's stories in this book were handwritten. However, he didn't leave them in a nicely planned out order, nor in a pile or file folder. His handwriting needed to be deciphered, as well. Bob had a black three-ring loose leaf 6 X 8 notebook that he wrote in, from time to time, nothing in order, just wrote where ever the book fell open at a blank page. Many of the dates and events are from this book. This book was originally both Gennevieve's, his wife, and Bob's. Their addresses, budgets and World War II war ration numbers for us all were in there. Bob also wrote on backs of envelopes, or on the inside covers of empty stationery tablets, and even in an old school notebook of Nejl's which Bob turned upside down and wrote in, between the lines. Bob told us that his writings were left scattered around where he threw it in a box for us to gather up and put into book form, after he was dead. He had most of it written. Nothing has been changed in Bob's writings. His stories are left as he wrote them, as this is history in the making. Bob's colorful figures of speech and expressions are as Bob wrote them.

Bob said, "It seemed like if anything historical happened, I was there. Something that changed the history of the United States of America, I was there, like the battle at Columbus, New Mexico."

The many articles, by Bob, on the horses were written over a period of years as the Spanish Mustang Registry grew. The first 32 years of my own life were spent on the Cayuse Ranch working with Bob Brislawn, helping to write his stories, the ranch work and the search for the pure horses for the Spanish Mustang Registry. It has been over forty years since 1976 when Bob Brislawn gave me the poem, 'The Rolling Stone' to use when I wrote the book on his life. I answered that I wasn't writing a book... but I have been gathering his stories ever since. These years have been spent attempting to gather up, and focusing on, putting this material in sequence like a journal or diary, as to dates. Then, to create continuity, I "filled in the gaps" between Bob's writings, adding what I know about the horses and the people who rode them. None of the names mentioned in this book were changed to protect the innocent and the privacy of the individuals involved. There are a lot of people who were not mentioned, who should have been. I started out to include everyone in one book but some others need a book of their own. Since there is too much material for one book, watch for a series of books. Thank you to my family and all others who helped as without their help this book could not have been possible. Someone said, "The only thing better than a lie, is a true story no one will believe". Happy reading as Bob Brislawn comes riding into your life...

       ---Dipper

Section Two

Wheat Ranch and Boyhood Days

Prologue by Bob

Should I write the prologue to my own stories - lies? Well, these are no lies - but just the natural happenings of anyone born in 1890, when the world was still young and man was still an adventurer and going out looking for Romance. Gold mining, horse racing, mustanging, railroad building, cowboying, lumberjacking, freighting; anything with plenty of action. I was shining shoes in a barber shop in 1901. Still old buffalo hunters, packers, and teamsters from the old Indian fighting 7th around. While waiting for a haircut they would get a shine and I would take plenty of time so to ask them a million questions; and from some, a lot of frontier information. Every boy looking for adventure. The banker's sons, the miller's sons, the merchants' sons, and all the town kids wanting to get out to the ranches, to the mines, and to the woods. Going out harvesting, out railroad building, or mining. The merchants, bankers, butchers, in fact most all business men, had been freighters, cowmen, stagedrivers, prospectors, before settling to the quiet life.

When in the early 1900's one graduated from high school, he was considered educated and could get any job in banks or government departments. My brother, Ferdinand, went into the hometown bank. No fun there. Next thing I knew, someone said, "I see your brother Ferdie driving a six-horse team down Main Street".

I went out to Montana to work for the Topographic Survey as recorder with chance to be Topographic Engineer. The packer quit, so I say, "No fun in being a map maker, give me the mules and ponies".

Gene Miller didn't want his Dad's hardware business. Too tame for him. Gene goes to the woods. In a year he's home for a visit. I see him on the corner talking to a bunch of farmers. He was something to see in his stagged off pants, caulked laced boots, red and blue wool socks turned down over the tops of the boots, red and yellow stagehand shirt and slouch hat. All his old school chums, both girls and boys, coming by. Gene was quite the hero. Well, the Lumber Jacks are gone. Been mechanized, even to oxfords. I just came back from Spokane (1964); I say to my sister Alice, 'I am going down on Front Street to see a Lumber Jack". Alice says, "You are as antedated as they. No more river pigs or lumber jacks". I guess they are loggers now. The Lumber Jack and River Pig was, I dare say, as much of America as the cowboy,

20

but no dime novels to build him up, So... We lived from the horse days to the missile days, but when the missile days are gone will everyone be wearing Missile Man's clothes like all are wearing cowboy clothes today? ---Bob

November 18, 1890

November 18, 1890; I was born in Sprague, Washington, Lincoln County, one night when I was young. It seemed the good Lord kept us old timers moving. My grand parents came from Ireland in the Potato Famine in 1848 to America. My Dad, Fir Brislawn, came to the Oregon and Washington Country in the seventies. He came there with a new suit and a mule-shoe mustache. Me in 1890...with no clothes. My mother came from Ireland. She died when I was seven; I lived, until I was 11, with my Uncle Mat and Aunt Mary on a cow and wheat ranch seven miles north of Sprague.

My Dad ran a wheat warehouse in Sprague, and he and I batched most of the time after I was eleven until I finished high school in 1912. I working in a barber shop as shoe-shiner and janitor from 6 a.m. until 9 p.m. and on Saturday from 6 a.m. until 2 a.m. Sunday, as Barber shops in those days closed at 12 a.m. Saturday night. When I was 13, I went to Moeler Barber College in Spokane to learn the barber trade, Came back to Sprague, as it were, to Charlie Ivy's and he gave me an extra barber chair. I continued shining shoes, washing bath tubs, and barbering when I could find a customer brave enough to let me shave him. This life was too confining so I became anemic. Need get out in the country, so would go harvesting, driving derrick, header box, or just pulling weeds out of the wheat, at one dollar and found. ---Bob

Cow-Herd

While the bannack bakes I will drop you a line, Al... It all happened in our time from the wheel to the Bomb. Fifty years ago, Al, you were taking the town milk cow herd out to graze, at $5.00 per month. Picking them up in the morning and bringing each back to her corral at night. I can close my eyes, Al, and see you on that little roan cayuse, agoing on the run, getting those milk cows bunched to take to Hiedo flats and prairie knolls in that old scab rock country. Well, Al, we are a long way from the `town herd'. Modern work, even to tie-downs on cowhorses, to braking a colt at two and really riding him. Emmett wants a five year old so can `really ride him' without making a dead headed stumblebum out of him. One thing sure, we old mossy horns are not forced to follow this modern trend. ---Bob

Shepherd Black and Tan

"Like the mustangs," says my old friend Gilbert Jones,

"the old Shepherd Black and Tan has been restored." The old sheep dog was history and tradition, first brought to England by the Danes when they over ran the country (12th century?) Then to America with the colonies, and later along with the wagons to the Great North West in 1850. But like the mustangs they were all but extincted due to show and ribbon animals.

Well this isn't what I came out here under the tree to write. After dinner as per usual the men would take 5 out on the lawn in front of the big ranch house, and, of course, we two little boys would be around to listen to the talk. Mat looks down the lane and says: "Look, here comes old Shep with a can in his mouth." Shep jumps the yard fence and comes over to Mat. Lays the can at Mat's feet and backs off and wags his tail. Mat reaches and picks up the can. The lid is pushed in a little so Mat takes his knife and pulls the lid up and out jumps a ground squirrel. Now you scientists say a dog can't think? OK. But a Black and Tan Shepherd can. That was our chief fun. Having Shep and Turk dig out squirrels on the prairie. The wheat ranch at that time paid a bounty of a cent a squirrel. This in Washington in 1910. ---Bob

Gold

Gold discovered in the Klondikes in 1898, said to be an Indian name Thron Diuck, but pronounced Klondike. I was eight years old at the time. George Kesler, our neighbor, and wife lived near by on Slasherville. I remember George well, he was five foot nothing but a rugged little man. When the big excitement started he decided to go get rich. I can shut my eyes and see little George packing up a bay pony with every thing from a shovel to frying pan. His old slick A fork saddle on a little roan Indian pony and what he couldn't get on the pack horse he tied somewhere on his saddle pony, and kissed Mrs. Kesler good bye. She crying, then was brave as he got on his pony. She smiles, said, "God go with you and bring back a big nugget for Fir (my Dad)". He did, a $5.00 one. He rode to Alaska. What was time in those days. Another man came along headed for the Klondikes. He was horseless. Had a big New Foundland dog, tan and white, hitched to a little wagon a lot like kids play with only really rugged, a homemade affair. The dog pulling a load and the man walking. He had a pair of runners tied over the load for if and when he hit snow he could change to a sled. Most people would go to Seattle and go by boat. Then hike into the Klondikes with pack on their backs. People with money had horses shipped along. I won't say horses for they at that time were all ponys, Indian stock. ---Bob

In the Mines

Talking of wages in the early 1900's; every mother's son from Dray driver to clerk and barber got 25 cents per hour or $15.00 per week. Nothing less than 10 hour day. Harvest wages from $3.00 to $7.00 with board, and as for room, one had the whole out doors. John Shearer came into the barber shop. I was at that time, 1910, barber, bootblack, and swamper. I shined his shoes. I said, lets go mining.

So we went to the Cour D' Alene and worked in the Bunker-Hill and Sullivan. Same was discovered by Phil O'Rouck. Ben Adams, also George Brislawn, each married one of his daughters. He sold the mine for $200,000.00 but died in the Sisters home in VanCouver. The money didn't last long; he was too big hearted.

One went to the mine boarding house (Beanery), asked if they would keep you until you got a job. If you seemed ok, they said, Ok. Then every evening when the mine foreman came up out of the mine and went to his office, you got in the rustling line. Maybe 50 men and the line would run through his office. When I came before him he says, "Are you a miner?" "No." "Mucker?" "No." "Ever work in a mine?" "No." "Report to Haggerty, 2000 ft. level in the morning." I worked on the outside at the Bunker-Hill and Sullivan Mine. But at Burke, Idaho in the Caladonia, where Haggerty was my shift boss, I worked at the 2000 foot level. Miners have it fine in this respect: fine big dry to hang one's wet clothes, baths and showers; so after work one takes off his digging clothes and no one knows him from the banker. I mined awhile, then got a job at Kellogg, Idaho freighting for the mines farther up the canyon. When fall came I went back to Sprague to work in the barber shop, Charlie Ivy's, and go to high school. ---Bob

1. NOTE BY DIPPER: Later, Ben Adams homesteaded close to where the Brislawns did, near Oshoto, Wyoming. George Brislawn is the son of Bob's uncle, Yankee Mike Brislawn.

Building the North Coast Railroad

The North Coast railroad was building through in 1908. I and Bill Monahan decide to try that. Rolled our blankets and went out eight miles to where the road was being constructed. Got a job bucking ties. That means carrying them to where they are needed; maybe sometimes 100 yards from where they were unloaded to the end of the line.

The boss or foreman was a hard looking old boy, maybe 35. Big six guns strapped around him. We ate in a box car and slept in same. Everybody lousey and as for meals, when the gong sounded--drop everything and run or else go hungry. Seen men, in order not to be beat out of their pie, to put it in their coffee cup with their coffee. One day I guess the boss didn't like the way my partner, Bill, combed his hair, anyway he said go to the pay car and get your time. We at that time were carrying ties, two men to a tie. These ties were heavy oak ties and I was left to carry a tie alone. Later on the boss says to me, "Where is your partner?" I say, "You fired him." So the rest of the day I carried ties alone. Just stood them on end and let them fall on my shoulder. That night I decided to go with Bill. I knew all I cared to learn as to building railroads. ---Bob

Wheat Ranch Day's Schedule

Mules in the South, horses in the North and West. On the wheat ranch where I was raised, likely 40 or more horses in the stable. No one had less than 4 - 7 on two bottom gang plow, ten on three bottom plows. At 5 o'clock, up and feed your horses each a gallon of grain and all the hay they could eat, harness them, clean out behind them. Go to breakfast at 6. Take horses out at 7, and go to the field. 11:30 unhitch and come in, water horses and put them in stable, feed them gallon of grain and the hay. Go to dinner. One o'clock, take teams out. 5:30 unhitch. Go to Stable, take off harness, feed gallon grain and manger full of hay. Go to Supper. In the South it was easier: Put the mules in the wire corral or lot, throw in cornstalks with corn on, or cane. This once a day, at night. Noon, eat your lunch at work. Let the mules stay in their traces. ---Bob

Dress as Good as You Should

You are right, Al. It does look like I am being dressed for `Del Monte' with these pants up here in the sticks. And that brings back memories of my cousin, Mark, and the wheat ranch where we were raised. Mark was great for pulling a fast one. When he would come home to the ranch from College he would have an old suit that was passed College wear. So he would don same, get his ten horses on the three bottom gang, and be plowing along side of his cousins; their wheat ranch joined. When they met along the fence they would stop to talk. Mark would say, "You guys don't dress as good as you should for rich wheat ranchers." This sure, as Mark would say, pulled their corks. ---Bob

Section III

Beginning with the Survey

Beginning of 30 Years

The school vacation of 1911 I got a job with Mr. John Blackburn, United States Geological Survey, Topographic Branch, at DeBorgia, Montana, Bitterroot Mountains. I broke a few ponies and then we outfitted out of there, camping at the Hogan Ranch while we were getting outfitted. Ed Brannon ran the general store at DeBorgia. I started  as a recorder but the packer quit so I was put on as packer. $50 per month, fine job. All horses Indian ponies; the best pack animals to me, not but what the small Spanish mules were very good. Just lead the old bell mare and the rest would follow. When the cook and I moved camp we never lead any pack horses. Would like to see a pack train of these modern horses turned loose. Believe a few packs would be scattered. ---Bob .

Doctor Bittner and the Reems Boys

Sprague, Washington, 1911: Bob was in failing health at the age of 20 because of the indoor work he did. 6 a.m. until 9 a.m. then schooling for the day, then working in the barber shop until midnight and on Saturday nights until 2 a.m. Sunday. Spring of 1911 before school was out Doctor Bittner told Bob that there was no hope, that he could give Pepsin to Bob and that it would help but not cure his trouble. Bob should look at the Reems boys, they worked outside and cut logs with a two-man hand saw. They never had indigestion nor were they ever sick. When school was out that spring, Bob pulled out, hit for the great out-of-doors, and he started work with the United States Geological Survey, Topograghic Branch on May 25, 1911. When it all begin there were 10 men and 25 horses at DeBorgia, Montana. Packer made $50.00 per month and recorder only $40.00. ---Nejl and Dipper

That Kid Can't Pack

I was packing out of Avery, Idaho for the USGS-TB in 1911. Mr. John Blackburn, Chief of Party. I originally came up to record, but Bert Kelly, the packer, decided it was easier to go down to Plumber and drive a mower. Some of the old timers said, "That kid can't pack." But the Chief like all the old topographers could do anything from drawing contours to shoeing a mule. So got a few lessons in packing from him, also from an old prospector who had a claim near our camp, and the little mules and Indian ponies were perfect little pack animals; if a pack slipped they just waited for you to come back to fix it. They usually trailed along behind. Never tied together like these modern days. Nor did one have pack equipment like today. Just a swing rope, 1/2 inch, and a 34 foot, 1/2 or 5/8 inch, lash rope.

Packed up the St. Joe River, then up to the Three Sisters and on over into the Clearwater River country, 35 or 40 miles. One day trip in, two out. Wages $40 to $50 for packers, rodman and recorders. The Chief maybe $125. Same each per day in camp for chuck (per diam).

I being sent for supplies, camped 15 miles up the St. Joe the first night coming back to camp. The Chief said the ponies would not leave me so I turned them loose. No hobbles. Lots of bear along the river and I had lots of good eats. I didn't know anything about bears, what they might do, so I piled up the groceries, made my bed beside them, and went to sleep. Woke up dreaming a bear was licking my face. I really came out of it and grabbed for the axe, same I had laid by my bed. It was just a big bull frog that had hopped on my face. So I see it's nothing and can hear no bell. Starts out for to look see. They had pulled out because I didn't have them all, and some had buddies at camp.

They crossed the St. Joe and headed up the trail to the Three Sisters. Waded the river and climbed to top, elevation 8000 feet. They were eating along the trail. 5000 feet climb to get them as the river is 3000 feet. So when I got to camp a day late the Chief says, "Did you go on a spree?".

When the recorder left for school that fall we were 35 miles out of Avery, Chief says, "You can take Tip in and get the mail and groceries". Tip says, "Will you get to Avery in time for me to catch the four o'clock train?" "Can't do it, I says, its seven now and I have to get the ponies, and can't get away before eight". So Tip decided to walk the 35 miles and I could ship his bed roll. But Tip couldn't find his hat. The Chief said, "Likely in your hurry you rolled it in your bed". He had. Then the Chief said, "Maybe you could take the drill, single jack, cement, and canteen, and put in a bench mark on your way in, Tip". Tip did and he caught the train at four. I picked up the canteen, drill, and single jack on the way back. Taking an hour out for putting in the bench mark, Tip made the 35 miles in less than seven hours. ---Bob

Innocents Abroad

That was my last trip to Avery. The Chief, Mr. Blackburn had the mail forewarded to Superior, Montana on the Clark Fork of the Columbia, as we were to move over that away, same we did. So here goes innocents aboard a Mustang going from our new camp to Superior.

Climbed out over the divide and down the slope to the Superior Valley. Trail finally hit an old logging road down the slope, then a country road up the valley, down draws, and over ridges. Beautiful country. Ranches along the valley. I notice some dust, then a rider tops a ridge. When the rider got nearer, next ridge, looked like a kid, but sure riding. Then, Whoa Horses. I meet head on a beautiful young lady on a little brown pony and holding up a bottle of milk like a prize.

I said, "Hello, you are late milking".

She said, "Where did you come from?"

I told her.

She say, "Ma sent me to town for the mail and a bottle of milk".

"Where do you live?" I ask.

"See those ranch buildings up there? Come up and see me tonight."

"Ok, if I can get around; supplies bought and so forth."

She, "What do you mean, so forth?"

"Well, I won't get drunk."

Well, I managed to get things in shape. The stores in those days, 1911, had corrals for pack outfit and feed. After supper I took the Kit horse and rode to the ranch.

"Boy", I say, "Kit, we are just in time for the dance".

So I put Kit in the corral, set on the corral looking things over. It was dark. A man coming by says, "Well, Kid, you might as well come on in and get your feet wet".

He went on in and I followed up on the porch. Could see three couples dancing, so I knocks. Someone opened the door. I said, "I was invited here by a young lady".

The young lady was dancing but when she saw me, dropped her partner, rushed over to me and says, "Glad you came", and took me into a room. An old lady laying on a bed. "Ma, this is the young man I met on the trail today". Then she left me.

So Ma and I soon got used to each other. I told her what I was doing, and she took me in like a son; showed me her six-gun. Said, "I am out on bonds for shooting a man that's been stealing my cows".

I said, "What is the dance for? Is it a wedding?"

"Yes, every night if any business", she say. "I run a house. Can't make a living since my husband died. Why not come and work for me this winter?"

Then my girl came in and say, "Come with me". There on a bench at a table sat Robinson Crusoe and Friday; two packers for the trail crew over on the Clearwater. They were drinking bottle beer. I dance and talk to this girl. I said, "What are you doing here?"

"Making money to go to college on".

"No," I said, "I will buy four bottles of beer and here is a five to get the Sheepskin with. So let us old packers drink to your Education".

Then I slip out to the corral and Kit. Back in town, I went to an old house near the store with bed in same. After awhile I heard noise out in front so I looked and there was Robinson Crusoe and Friday. Friday piling up rocks in the street. So I put on my pants and boots and went out. "You old river pigs are making too much noise", I said, "come to bed".

"No", says Friday. "After you left, Mrs. Johnson, the horse shoer's wife came up to the whore house and asked if her husband was there and someone said he was and he will sure think it was me. So I will wait here until he comes along. If I don't, he will find me in the morning. If I am going to get licked, I want to get licked now, not in the morning. And if he licks me there won't be a rock left in the street."

But I and old man Robinson Crusoe, as he was called, finally got Friday to bed. This girl went to college, afterward married an attorney-at-Law in Spokane. This last from a girl in Wyoming that used to go out to Ma's ranch to cook, with no names mentioned. Her name was Goldie, and Ma got out of the shooting scrape. Duncan Small will remember all of this. He was raised in that country and was cook for the Survey at that time. ---Bob

Turn 'er Muzzle Up the Hill

When we finished that survey we went to DeBorgia, Montana to map in the Bitterroots. Stopped over in Spokane to visit my sister, Alice.

I went out from Plains, Montana to where the Survey horses were pastured. I and the recorder took them to DeBorgia, 65 miles in one day. They needed no conditioning. Whenever one of those Indian ponies was in good flesh he was `in fix' and ready for a 75 mile ride. Too much draft or something in today's horse. Maybe have too many lumbar vertebra.

The fall before, I had trailed the horses to Plains and was trying to get a ride back to Paradise, Montana, Someone said the doctor goes over every day, so looked up the doctor. He says ok.

Road above the Clark Fork is narrow and 300 feet above the river. We came around a curve and face to face with a young man and his sweetheart. The young man had that old Ford at top speed. What did he do? Just turned her nose up the side of the mountain, we slipped by and he rolled back into the road. Now this doctor was furious and sure gave that young man a tongue lashing. I thought he should give him a `medal of reward' for using his head and being brave by turning up the side of the mountain. If he hadn't we all could have made the river. Anyway, wherever that boy is today, to me he is a hero. ---Bob

NOTE: The following is John E. Blackburn's Obiturary--from a yellowed newspaper clipping, without a date. (Dipper Brislawn October 1983.)

John E Blackburn, Western Pioneer and Surveyor

John E. Blackburn, retired Geological Survey Topographic Engineer who took part in the survey's first sectionizing and mapping of Indian Territory died Saturday at Mount Alto Hospital. He was 80. Born in Missouri he spent his first 10 years In Texas. His family had taken him in a covered wagon. His father, a Confederate soldier, and mother, both died when he was 3. From the age of 10 until he was 20, he lived in Indian Territory near McAlester, Oklahoma. Mr. Blackburn was an ORIGINAL SOONER as he took part in the Stampede in 1891 and 1892 on the Cherokee strip when Indian land was opened to the white man. Mr. Blackburn got in the race and drove his claim stake into the ground, but he couldn't legally hold it because he was under age, his wife said. Mr. Blackburn went to Pullman College and began work for the Geological Survey in 1895. He was a moundsman (Made mounds of dirt in the earth at given distances), packed provisions on mules and was a teamster when Indian Territory was sectioned and mapped. In 1910 he became an assistant topographer. Mr. Blackburn once was caught in a big forest fire while leading a surveying party in the Bitterroot Mountains on the Idaho-Montana border. They were saved when the wind changed. John E. Blackburn, retired twice. When he first retired in 1935 he had mapped and helped map 72 quadrangle maps of 19 different States. In 1942 he was reappointed to the survey for emergency mapping, retiring in 1947. Since then he had done private surveying in Falls Church, Virginia, where he lived. John E. Blackburn was an Army Engineer during World War I and held a captain's commission in the Army Reserve.

<> If a person learns everything his teachers know and a little bit more -- as the saying goes... Just look at the life of John E. Blackburn and the opportunity Bob had for learning from him. Quoting Bob, "Blackburn was my teacher". ---Dipper

Trapped in That Canyon Inferno, Idaho 1911

Bob Brislawn was among the surveying crew of Chief of Party, John E. Blackburn, in the Bitterroot Range of the Rocky Mountains, when they were caught in that forest fire, with no way out of a box canyon. When the fire broke out the survey crew were among those who volunteered their help. Not knowing the area they were pushed along ahead of the fire until they were in a box canyon with lots of rocks and boulders among the trees. The smoke was so heavy they covered their faces with the neckerchiefs they always wore around their necks--red bandana folded into a triangle then tied with a square knot in front, with a honda to slip up to tighten around the neck. While trailing cattle herds, during dust or fires, the men pulled the scarfs around and covered their faces bandit-fashion to filter the dust, smoke and ashes from the air. (Bob's honda was ivory colored. In later years after he Homesteaded in Wyoming he carved his `N Spear' Brand on it. I still have this honda.) The canyon walls were too steep for them to climb out; hemming them in on three sides with the fire on the other side, so no way out...they all thought this was the end for them (that they were as good as dead) so each person began asking God's forgiveness for all the wrong that they had done and were making their peace with God. The fire was so hot that anything metal was burning them. The men were throwing away their Medals, Crucifixes, watches, and Wedding Rings. Even the Medals worn for protection against all evil were burning them. Bob had on a Brown Scapular. He wore one of these Brown Scapulars all of his life. (A Scapular is a cloth medal and is a symbol associated with "garments" or a cloak" of grace and love. The Scapular represents the love and protection of our Heavenly Mother Mary.) The fire had pushed them to the end of the box canyon. There was no way out. The walls were to steep to climb out. The heat was so intense it was burning their faces and hands. They had covered their faces with scarves, and finally pulled their hats down over their faces hoping to breathe the last good air that might be trapped in the crown. They were lying on the ground to try to get below the smoke, heat and fire. At the last minute the wind changed -- blowing the fire and smoke away from them, saving them all! ---Dipper

Nez Perce Fishing Horse

I packed out of Plains, Montana. Was crossing the Clark Fork, riding the Chief's saddle pony, Molly. The mules and ponies following. Two lumber jacks coming along the trail. A tree on each side of the river had fell together for a foot bridge. The young lumber jack wasn't feeling any pain but the old boy was loaded, really staggering along. The young man walked the logs. The old boy stopped when he got to the river, took a good look at the logs, then slid off the bank, grabbed one of the Indian ponies by the tail and was pulled across. He wasn't drunk. . . he might be staggering but his head was clear. Nez Perce Indians fishing in the river. They had developed a fishing horse. They speared, snared, and line fished off their ponies, riding them out in the steams. Mostly horses of white or white and red spots. Likely these colors the fish could see? They snared with a real thin copper wire on the end of a pole. ---Bob

1912 High School Graduation

Class of 1912, Sprague, Washington, May 17th to 22nd
Class Motto: Die Arbeite besiegt alles. Class Flower: White Carnation
Class Colors: Blue amd White
Robert E. Brislawn: Oration
* * * * * * * * * * *

Graduating Class:

Bevla M. Williams --- English Course

Ella B. Fish --- Scientific Course

Amy N. Melville --- Classical Course

Alta I. Mills --- Scientific Course

Robert E. Brislawn --- Scientific Course

William J. McDonald --- Scientific Course

Bob graduated from high school at the age of 21; at the time when high school was the equivalent of a college degree of today. A high school graduate was considered educated so could go into any field of work. The Class Motto: Die Arbeite besiegt alles. The Work conquers all. In later years Bob often commented on that Motto. "How true it is," he said.

He proved it true with the saving of the Spanish Horse and the registry to preserve those horses." Bob was the Orator and made his speech about the fact that the World would be at peace during the 20th century as people were more educated so there would not be WARS! Bob often commented on this during all the wars we did have. "How wrong I was," he said. ---Dipper

Lame Horse

Bakers, butchers, barbers, and doctors, lawyers, merchants and thieves were all horsemen in 1912. Major Gerdine, Topographic Chief of the United States Geological Survey, came out from Washington D C to make visits to the different camps.

He got off the train in DeBorgia, Montana. Asked at the saloon and hotel as to where Mr. Blackburn's party was, and was told out twenty miles on Packsaddle Creek. So he manage for a horse and starts out. Gets to our camp, but we had moved on to Greyback, high up in the Bitterroots. He looks around and finds our trail and keeps acoming, camping out that night. At the camp the Chief says, "Maybe you best go to DeBorgia for supplies, and I will send a letter to be held at the post office for Gerdine. He could be coming". I come around a bend in the trail and run right into the Major. He says, "Sure glad to see you". Then I notice a white handkerchief tied around his horse's front canon. He said, "This isn't an Indian pony, he is thoroughbred and wasn't raised here, so hurt his leg; tore a tendon loose. I've been keeping a wet cloth on it to keep the swelling down".

I said, "What will I do now?"

"I suppose you just as well go get the supplies for I will stay around a few days.

And this horse will likely be ok by then". In the thirty years I packed for the Survey we never had a horse crippled, except some thoroughbred horses that we had in later years. ---Bob

33 Horses on the Combine Harvester

I was freighting in the Coeur d'Alene in 1914. Had a card from my cousin Mark saying, "Sorry you did not come by on your way, but hope you can make it here to Pullman when you pull in this fall", as the first of July I had a job as packer with John Blackburn, Chief of Party, Topographic Branch, mapping in the Bitterroots.

When I got to the State College in Pullman that fall, Mark was telling me the fun he had instead of going home to the wheat ranch at Sprague, Washington to drive the 33 horses on the Combine Harvester. He said, "I decided to go to the woods and try lumber. So I goes to Spokane, goes down on Front Street and buys me a $50 outfit, from slouch hat to kaulked boots. Then goes up on Riverside where all the elites would be walking and shopping. Met several of the college boys and girls and gives them `Hi, John', or `Hi, Mae'. It sure got the girls, and they passed me up like a dirty shirt. But I sure looked them down. I sure pulled their corks." "The boys laughed it off and said, `Wish I could be with you, Mark'." Mark worked in the woods that summer.

The last time I saw Mark he and his two sons came by where I was packing in Colorado. Mark a major in the army then. He says, "I put in a hell of a time on the ranch this summer. No one there but Mike (his Brother) and Jim McCaffry and a tractor. (Mark had took leave.) Not like the good old days when there were 12 men on the ranch and 65 horses in the stable. Never again." ---Bob

On Foot from Seattle to Shasta Springs, California

In 1916 I took a job with Mr. John Blackburn of the United States Geological Survey to make a pamphlet for the Union Pacific (railroad company) from Seattle, Washington, to Shasta Springs, California, showing elevations and industries of each town. We could have had a speeder but too much bother as to trains so we walked. Average 20 miles per day, the 600 miles. In Roseburg, Oregon the Chief decided to lay over a day to do his office work, so we got a room each at the big hotel. Came down to the dining room, the waitress came over, handed us each a menu and said, "Hello, Bob". She was one of the waitresses of Arlington, Oregon that I used to row across the Columbia River. I never lived that down as to Mr. Blackburn. He went the limit and told everyone on the Survey that everyone in Oregon knows Bob...especially the ladies. ---Bob

Mr. Wilson's Hat

Mr. Wilson had a big ranch along the Snake with headquarters not far from Pittsburg Landing. Ferry across the Snake. He had a line camp up near the Oregon-Idaho border in the valley. He often packed salt to his cattle up on the top of the rim rock .... trail winding up along the ledges like a road with a 40 foot drop off or more in places to the side rock or rock slides. One day as Red Tate, one of his cowboys, was riding in to the line camp he noticed the pack mules and a saddle horse standing still on the trail to the rim, with the horse turned around, head down trail. But could not see the boss, so he rode up. As he turned a bend in the trail he looked down and saw Mr. Wilson a hundred feet below in the slide rock. So went down to the switch back and climbed up and got him. He was dead. Put him across his (Wilson's) saddle horse and went to the line camp. Mules with salt following along behind. Two of the other boys were at camp so they decided the best thing to do was for Bill to go to the ranch to notify Mrs. Wilson to meet Mr. Wilson at the Pittsburg Ferry, telling her that Mr. Wilson wanted her to bring his clothes and go to Lewiston with him. One of the other cowboys to take Mr. Wilson to the ferry to take him to Lewiston for burial.

At daylight they were all on their way. Bill got to the ranch, told Mrs. Wilson. "While you are getting ready I will get you a horse to meet the ferry at 10 o'clock". Bill came back with the horse and Mrs. Wilson was all ready, except she couldn't find Mr. Wilson's hat. Now one of the older cowboys at the line camp had said, "Now, Billie, try to break the news really gentle to Mrs. Wilson". Mrs. Wilson kept looking for his hat and time was getting short to make the ride to the river to catch the ferry boat. So Billie finally say, "Mrs. Wilson, just let the hat go. Mr. Wilson won't need his hat where he is going". She said, "What?" Then Billie told her.

Our party broke up early that year. My brother, Frank went

with Mr. Ogle and some of the rest to map the Green River and I took the camp and horses to Driggs, Idaho to Mr. Burchard and Andrews for work up the North Fork of the Salmon, and the Salmon River country in general useing Triangulation.

The old Molly mare, so old we only lead her so the others would follow as well as stay around camp, finally gave it up so we left her with a little homesteader. Good grass and water. He was all alone, say she be company and maybe could carry in a deer for him. So. ---Bob

Note of Interest:

On November 15, 1986 when Uncle Frank was staying with us before he died, he told me: "While surveying on the Green (River) it was on the Yampa Canyon Fork, a branch of the Green". "We went nearly all the way down it to Vernal, Utah."

Also, Uncle Frank told me , "While working on the Green, we worked with sons or grandsons of the early explorers or surveyors, not just there but all over the West. `Pike is one of those. `No Fish' is another." (I looked up `Pike' in The World Book Encyclopdia and found that Albert Pike would be a descendant of Zebulon Montgomery Pike, 1779-1813, an American general and explorer. In Colorado, Pike's Peak is named after Zebulon Pike.) ---Dipper

Who's Guilty?

Is my friend "Goldie", the milkmaid guilty, or my boyhood friend, Bill McDonald, guilty? Here is his story.

Bill McDonald, my schoolchum, and I decided we would go to college. This in 1916. We graduated from high school in 1912. I had saved a thousand dollars by working on ranches, survey, and mines, and so forth. Bill was working in the Coeur d'Alene, big mining region of Idaho, at Mullin in the mines. But when fall came and almost time to go to college at Pullman, he hadn't saved any money.

So, Idaho dry, Montana wet. He needed a quick stake so one way out. Over the mountain divide between the two states them days there were no highways, just roads, but cars using them going over from Mullin, Idaho to Saltese or DeBorgia. The cars would drag a pole behind them so when they stopped on the grade their car would roll back on it. So on the top of the divide was a world of poles. Bill and his miner friends, of course, would go over to the Montana side quite often, so really knew the roads and side roads. Bill decided he was going to college so took a car, went over to the Montana side, got a load of whisky. Coming back over the divide Bill knew all the side roads. If he seen the lights of a car coming he pulled off. He sold the whisky at a profit of $300, at least enough to get started, and one could always work some of the way at college. Well, Bill went to Pullman for awhile, until Christmas, studying Veterinarian. I took my money and went homesteading in Wyoming, fall of 1916. ---Bob

Captain McDonald

When I see an old picture of an old survey party it just seems like yesterday; the world was still young in 1916. If ever a man was glad to meet me, it was Captain McDonald. I got a letter from Mr. Gerdine, Chief Topographic Engineer, Washington, D.C. for me to pick up 11 head of public animals at the Hogg Ranch near Yakima, Washington and report same to Harry L. McDonald, Prosser, Washington. Also in same mail a telegram from my brother F. L. for Dad and I to meet him in Billings, Montana as he had located good Homestead lands in Wyoming and to come at once. So, I telegramed Mr. Gerdine that, `OK but will be a few days late.' Mr. McDonald hurried to Prosser, just to sit and twiddle his thumbs until I arrived. He had passed up his hometown as well as his Sweetheart to be on time and not been notified that I would be late. So when I did arrive with the horses he said, "I am CERTAINLY glad to meet you!" ---R. E. (Bob) Brislawn

Section Four

Homesteading Required Outside Income.

Spring of 1916

Spring of 1916, Sprague, Washington: Rarey Fir, Ferdie and Bob were all ready to go homesteading in Lake County, Oregon, when they went to a dance and Mrs. Doc Baker was there; she told them how great Wyoming was and how good the crops grew. Her and her husband, a Veternarian, had homesteaded out in Wyoming. Rarey Fir, Ferdie, and Bob Brislawn with Bill McDonald and Hoodemaker came out in May to see.

They all rented horses from Zimmerschied's, to ride while looking at land to homestead. The horses might have been rented from John Zimmerschied's Livery Stable, on Cabin Creek, near Carlile, Wyoming. That huge old barn/stable was just over the timbered ridge from the Carlile Store. Jim Barrett of the Land Office, in the courthouse, Sundance, Wyoming showed them the land near Oshoto.

Later, Uncle Frank said, "They fell for it like a ton of bricks." Other people wanted that land but thought that the D Ranch owned it. There had been some kind of cover up in the land office for Driskill of the D Ranch but Jim Barrett knew that the land was still available for homesteading when he showed it to the three Brislawns, Bill McDonald and Hoodemaker.

Rarey Fir was riding a red roan horse that bucked all over the flat. Rarey Fir had a terrible ride and was beat up badly because his belt, or his chap's belt, was hooked over the saddle horn so he couldn't get it loose. That is the reason Rarey Fir homesteaded were he did. They filed the homestead papers on the 12th of May 1916, then returned to Sprague, Washington.

They came back in the Fall of 1916 in a boxcar with some household goods, two Holstein heifer calves, four horses and a Buggy for Mrs. Baker. A team, Sprague and McKinty, were two of those horses. "The Bug" was another one of the four horses that were brought from Sprague, Washington. At least Bob got her right away if she didn't come with them. Uncle Frank named her "The Bug" because of the way she would lay down on her stomach to crawl under fences, going any place she wanted that way. Emmett still has a descendant of "The Bug".

When Mrs. `Doc' Baker led Rarey Fir, Ferdie and Bob out to Oshoto homesteading they had a wagon to bring for themselves. When Mrs. Baker asked them to bring a buggy for her, they did. That didn't leave room in the railroad train's boxcar (or immigrant-car as it was called) for their own wagon. So they left their wagon behind in Sprague, Washington. After they arrived in Moorcroft, Wyoming, they managed for a cart to haul their belongings the 30 miles out on the D Road to Short Prong of Prairie Creek, the headwaters of the Little Missouri River near Oshoto, Wyoming, where they homesteaded. This cart had axles that were too wide, so that the wheels didn't track the same as other wagons; at this time the D Road was only a pair of ruts winding through the sagebrush and sod, so that one side of the cart was out on the sod and sagebrush making it terribly rough riding. Later, they bounced along to go to Moorcroft after supplies. This cart was eventually shortened so it would `track' okay. It was still there at Uncle Frank's place at the time of this writing.

Bob dug all the postholes by hand in one day on quarter mile of fence line on Farey Firs homestead, because the ground was so sandy and soft...for that two-wire fence. The "D" Road was named after the Driskills who had trailed so many thousands of longhorn cattle from Texas in the late 1800's on the Texas Trail. The tracks these trailherds left can still be seen today. Of course, the land that the Brislawns filed on and homesteaded was used and claimed for grazing by the `D' Ranch because of the good watering holes, ever since they first trailed the longhorns up the trail from Texas.

After Bob had his shack built near the major watering hole that the D Ranch claimed, a bunch of D Riders came to tell Bob he had to get off his homestead as the D Ranch considered this 'open-range'; this land and waterhole was their property. Bob was outside his shack chopping fire-wood when he saw them coming with their 6-guns strapped on and with serious expressions to their faces...so Bob started in by waving and hollering, "Hello, you boys sure ride good horses." Bob continued talking in his rapid fire pace so the cowboys never got a chance to tell him what they came for...they parted friendly and remained friends after that. It was years later when they told Bob why they had come, that they had come to run him off...the D Range.

Rarey Fir Brislawn built most of the shacks around Oshoto for $25.00 a piece. He was so good at figuring how much lumber was needed for each shack that there wasn't many ends or pieces of boards left-over. Some of the homes were log; one was made with sod. (As told to me by Bob,.---Dipper)

The Texas Trail

Uncle Frank told me, when Jim Barrett showed the Brislawns that land out there that Driskil of the D Ranch was claiming as theirs; this Jess Driskel asked the Brislawns "Why did they want to Homestead because they all had a good education and could work anywhere but he didn't have a good education so needed that land."

Uncle Frank continued, "Most people who Homesteaded

did have an education: Dell Evans was an electrician and had a shop somewhere before he went homesteading. Bert Evans was County Commissioner for many years. Also Dr. Hoadley... Jess Driskel came up the trail with the longhorns. When he was 16 years old he was the trail boss - so he was far from dumb!

"Revenuers are Coming"

Uncle Framk told me about Prohibition....everyone had a Still --- most of it (moonshine) was good.

Some people had stills in the wild plum thickets, they had to walk to it in a different spot each time so they wouldn't make a trail for the Revenuers to see leading into the thicket and not going on through.

One Homesteader had his pails of mash soaking along with the buckets of grain he was soaking for the pigs ... next to the fence of the pig-pen...with some other barrels and buckets of grain soaking for pig food. The sheriff or R.B.I. (Revenuers) stood right by the soaking grain in the buckets and barrels and never questioned it as moonshine/bootleg. They just thought it was pig-food.

When the Revenuers would come to the Sheriff's office to go out to check peoples places...the homesteaders would set up a relay- ride. One would ride to the next neighbor to tell him...then that man would ride to the next and so on until the whole area was informed about the Revenuers were coming so they could take the extra care to cover their tracks to their stills.

Trailherds Crossing the Creeks

Railroad town, Moorcroft, 30 miles. Usually went in with wagon and team, one day in, and out the next. If not loaded, a six hour trip, five miles per hour, but eight hours more better on one's team.

We shipped to Moorcroft from Washington in immigrant car. Our cousin, Mike Brislawn, gave Ferdie and I, each, a heifer calf. I never bought a cow; just hang on to her tail and by `25 had 20 cows, and later all that 3000 acres could run, all from the old black cow.

Now I just heard that the Quarter-horse brought the longhorns up the trail. Wonder as what those old trail drivers like Frank Morose, Joe Love, John Grould, or John O'Brien are laughing in their graves as to this. Frank Morose say, "Those ponies were sure fast and cowponies. When we came to a creek or river and the steers would not cross. two of us, one on each side of a steer; ponies just tall enough so we would hook a horn under in front of the saddle horn and drag the steer right along across the creek or bad place, with the boys behind pushing the rest right after us."

These Spanish ponies, also called Texas ponies, when turned loose in Wyoming or Montana for a couple years, even those eight years old, would grow a couple inches and put on 200 pounds. Originally they were 14 hands or under, 750 pounds, I was told by these old cowboys. ---Bob

Lost in a Blizzard

In 1916, Dad (Rarey Fir), Ferdie, and I went to North East Wyoming to homestead. 320 acres each. That year the Section Act passed and we took an additional 320, making a section of land out on the wild prairie, 10 miles to water, 10 miles to wood. Everyone built his shack near a water hole or spring along dry creeks, hauled wood from over across the Little Missouri River.

One day Ferdie and I went for a load of wood with two old mares that were brought from Washington by Hale Harreton. Lots of times, it seems, the blizzards hit then and do now, either nine in the morning or four at night. This time we had just crossed the river (it was dry), but good sledding, when she hit. Terrible wind and drifting snow. Ferdie say nothing to do but unhitch the mares, get on their backs, and see if they won't take us home. So ok, we start. Wind on right side of our faces. After riding a long time all at once wind in our face. Ferdie says, we must be lost. Pretty soon the mares stopped. We got off and there is a fence and gate, our gate. The mares hit the fence too far south and followed it up to the gate. We were camping in a homestead house of a Tonie Music. I only hope those brave mares are in the Horse Heaven. When one of those blizzards hit, it's dark already. The coldest I ever seen in Wyoming was 40 below. Sun shining bright, no wind, the side toward the sun warm, the other cold. Snow will melt and run off the buildings at 20 below on the sunny side. ---Bob

A Sunday School Picnic

New Mexico-Mexico Border: Bob and Ferdie left their Dad, Rarey Fir, alone to `hold the Fort', to carry on with the homesteads' improvements and brake out what was asked for the 1st year. (Homestead laws or rules were required to do each year so much plowing, ie: braking the sod, building and other improvements on the land they were filing on.).

Bob and Ferdie went to the New Mexico-Mexico Border with the Survey and General John Pershing to map for the War Department. Bob and Ferdie may have left Oshoto separately, a few days or weeks apart, as they were with different Survey Parties, working at different places. The New Mexico-Mexico Border was in the clutch of guerrilla warfare. Everyone wore guns in holsters and gun belts, strapped around their waists. Bob had his 45 pistol. Pancho Villa's guerrillas and small bands of bandits or Rurales were everywhere, plundering and burning. Food was scarce.

One Sunday a Fiesta was planned with a baseball game scheduled after the church service and picnic, with the United States Geological Survey Party playing against the local team. Bob had just ridden up to a ranch house as he was taking a local schoolteacher to this fiesta in the small town near by. The rancher with his wife and their small children had just left in their buggy for the celebration, when a band of 20 or more Rurales rode up. The Rurales flashed their white teeth in their smiles and talked that this would be an easy raid as there were only two people in the house. The signs were easy to read, only two saddled horses tied to the hitch-rack and the buggy gone; while they were heavily armed with guns and machetes, with ammunition belts strapped around waists, over one shoulder, and under the opposite arm as you see in pictures.

Bob decided he couldn't make a stand and try to shoot it out as they were greatly out-numbered. Even if the teacher loaded the guns while he did the shooting they wouldn't last long against the heavily armed guerrillas. They could run and hide but they would be searched for and if found would be killed. The best way would be go out alone and unarmed; they might not kill an unarmed man. The schoolteacher told him, "They won't hurt you. They are only hungry so give them food and they will go away."

Leaving his 45 pistol inside and telling the schoolteacher to stay out of sight and to keep quiet, Bob stepped out the door onto the wooden veranda to ask what they wanted. On the porch he was eye-level with the mounted Rurales. Bob spoke in English as he felt sure they would be killed if the Rurales knew he could understand their Spanish. He knew that by their gesturing, laughing and talking they were planning on killing them.

So with his Irish `gift-of-the-gab' he kept right on talking while the Rurales made it clear with their Spanish and hand signals that they were hungry and wanted all the FOOD on the place. Bob went back inside. Although he knew where the food was he took more time than needed banging doors and drawers while gathering up the food, acting as if he had to search for everything and to let the Rurales know what he was doing. There was some bacon, beans and flour out where it was easy to find but there was other food hidden.

Bob had helped the rancher hide some food in the barn a few days before...some hams and bacon were hidden in the oat bin. Not wanting the family to come home to nothing, as food was scarce, he only gave the food that was easy to find, hoping it would satisfy the Rurales so they would leave without killing them and burning the place. Bob helped the Rurales load up their horses with bacon, beans and flour, as he was an excellent packer, talking all the while and then stood to watch as they rode off... leaving without stealing saddle horses or plundering anything. As soon as the Rurales were out of sight Bob and his schoolteacher friend got on their horses and trotted off down the road to the town fiesta, where Bob took part in the baseball game as if he never looked death in the face a few hours earlier. "Death so often dashed aside," goes a poem by Rudyard Kipling (1865-1936). Death had once again dashed aside so Bob "could rise to fight another day." Bob said he "knew Pancho Villa." Perhaps this was the first of many meetings. ---Dipper

Pancho Villa

1916 Columbus, New Mexico: Pancho Villa, (1877-1923) was a Mexican chief who was seeking control of Mexico. There were many battles and raids with Rurales everywhere along the Border; the United States encouraged Villa at first, but President Woodrow Wilson turned to Carranza for President of Mexico.

Villa turned against the Americans in Mexico and across the border in America. According to the World Book Encyclopedia President Wilson sent U. S. Soldiers under the Command of General John J. Pershing (1860-1948) into Mexico in pursuit of Villa. Hampered by orders not to use the railroads, Pershing failed to capture Villa. All Mexicans, including President Carranza bitterly resented Pershing's expedition; the expedition was withdrawn in 1917. Pershing's failure to capture Villa made him a public character so when World War I broke out, President Wilson put him in charge of the American Expeditionary Forces.

Pershing insisted that the Amercian Army should fight independently and not be used to fill in the ranks of the battered Allied armies. Pershing's belief in fast moving troops, rather than troops dug into trenches, led to the early Victory of World War I.

Bob said, "when on the Border the Survey Party was guarded by the United States' 7th Cavalry when those combat troops were still mounted on horses." ---Dipper

A Welcoming Committee

Texas-Mexico Border area: Bob flagged down a train and was on his way into a town for supplies and groceries - when stepped off the train in a Texas Border town he had a welcoming committee of Rangers. Seems he looked like a notorious drug smuggler - the train's conductor had mistaken Bob for that smuggler and had telegraphed ahead to have him picked up. Bob didn't have identification with him at the time, things looked bad, but as luck would have it Bob saw someone there who knew him who just happened to be there in town who could identify him. ---Dipper

Billy The Kid's Gun

El Paso, Texas 1917: While Ferdie was working on a survey around El Paso he met John James, a shopkeeper, and his family. John James was murdered in a hold up of his store. Ferdie was working on a survey around Cottonwood, Arizona, at that time, but was called back to El Paso, by the James family, to help track down the killers. Ferdie was on the trail of the killers, with two Apache trackers, when he met up with the others, who were ahead of him, coming back.

The three outlaws had been captured and hung before Ferdie caught up with them. Later on, for his trouble in this search, Ferdie was given a Colt double action revolver that had belonged to John James, his future father-in-law. This small chrome plated pistol had been taken in trade by John James from William Bonney. The vital statistics are: Colt DA 41, Serial 23028. It was in Ferdie's possession, then of Gusher, Utah, until he took his last long ride. When Ferdie fell with a broken hip and was unable to take care of himself, he was put in a nursing home about 1974 and all of his prize possessions, including this pistol, were lost to us. ---Dipper

Anamus, New Mexico 1917

Nothing to do on Sunday in Anamus, when I was working for a survey party in 1917; so decided to run some wild burros into the windmill and ride them, so the boys, women and kids, and engineers all came down to the dirt-tank and windmill to watch the fun.

A young topographer thought it looked easy to ride a burro. Because everyone rode horses in those days, he thought he could ride a burro and he did ride it for awhile - rode it till it quit bucking - then he hollered `Whoopey' and kicked it. The Burro gave one good jump and throw him on the watering trough and broke a rib.

The nearest doctor was at an Army Post at Hatcheea, New Mexico, we flagged down the sunset limited and put him on the train. The Army doctor bandaged him up. Then he decided a few drinks of whiskey would help - but he got too many and got wild, he walked up and down the street thinking he could lick Old Mexico, and got too noisy even for that town. For want of a jail (no jail in those little border towns) they chained him to a telephone post, till he sobered up, with a good big log-chain and ankle-shackle.

A few days afterward he said to the teamster (being me), "When you go into Hatcheea to get supplies, see Sheriff Tomlin and give him this $10.00 as he has my watch".

I went down to the sheriff's house and found him in good shape - playing the piano and feeling pretty good. The sheriff said that our topographer got pretty loud so he fined him $10.00, as he was then the law west of El Paso, Texas, for disturbing the peace and as he didn't have the money he took his watch. ---Bob Brislawn, May 1957, Tijeras, New Mexico.

Note: This was written in Shorthand as Dad talked or told this story to me, when we were in New Mexico searching for the pure Spanish Horses. ---Dipper

Border Shootout

I was on the Mexican Border in 1917, teaming for United States Geological Survey, Topographic Branch. Mapping the border for the War Department as we were having trouble with Mexico. Lots of Rurales around. We were camped across the Rio Grande above El Paso, Texas. Had the 7th Cavalry to guard us while we slept.

Big party given for the survey men in El Paso, where Mrs. Captain Griffin stayed. So we took the buckboard and old Joke and Jake, two old veterans of the artillery. If one hollered or shot, they would charge. After the party the Captain said, "Boys, have you all got guns?" All we had was my 30-30 and one 45, so the Captain says, "It could be bad crossing over the river at Dickison Bridge. Here is a gun for each."

There were five of us so we starts for the feed yard to get the mules. I got a terrible nose bleed, so went into an all night drug store. The clerk started backing up when we came in, but Chuck says, "This man has only a nose bleed." He stuffs my nose with cotton dipped in adrenalin, and we goes out to the yard. Got the long eared darlings, and started out.

Just as we cross the river on the bridge, and start up the bank on south side, things broke loose. One hundred rurales lined the road. I hollered "Charge!", and Joke and Jack surely did nothing else, and the shooting started. We all were killed. Last I remember was I was ahold of the reins with one hand and still a-shooting... ---Bob

Section Five

World War I

He Didn't Wait to be Drafted. He was only a volunteer.

I came home from the Mexico Border in 1918, when the Survey pulled in from mapping the Border for the War Department, I being one of the Teamsters.

The War was on so I goes to Demming, New Mexico to enlist in the 24th Engineers, more or less the United States Geological Topographic outfit. My brother, Ferdie, was there, also to go. (Ferdie was with a different survey party mapping a different area and they had not seen each other for several months, but by coincidence they showed up at the Enlistment Office at the same time!) Ferdie said, "If you go I won't. I feel one of us should be home with Dad in Wyoming".

"O.K. you go", I said, "I haven't lost anything in France and will go home and cut posts to fence the ranch until I am called".

Ferdie enlisted as a Sergeant from Texas under General

John Pershing. (They both had cards from General Pershing to give to the Army so that they would be in General Pershing's outfit working for him over in France.)

When I got home Dad had Sprague and McKinty on the new sled (this in February) hauling hay off the open range of what would become Art Thompson's Homestead later. This was not more than two miles from our Homestead Cabins there on Prairie Creek. There were a thousand big Driskill Ranch steers on the Creek whit the fruit trees broke down and grass ate to the ground. But two miles away, in the hills, one could, as Dad said, "lose the mower, the wheat-grass so tall".

. So now with windmills everywhere from the Conservation Program, cows can eat it all and so there is very little wheat-grass anywhere. One thing sure in the days of open range before Uncle Sam built those reservoirs and windmills there were always plenty of grass for winter back in the hills. Reason being, too far from water, but not for mustangs who would go back in the rough 13 miles and stay several days without water, then come in on the run. (Signed) The Wyoming Kid

I started cutting posts. Ride over to woods the other side of the Little Missouri River. Cut a hundred and ride home the 10 miles. When the roads got good we would haul them. One day big Chinook, and river way over her banks when I got there, about the same time the Glover's School Teacher was coming along going home.

I said, "We could swim it if there wasn't so much brush

and logs acoming down. I will go back and stay with Clifford Emory".

She said, "Me, too". So back we go to his Cabin. No Clifford and just some old rusty hay for our ponies. But we stayed...and by daylight the river had gone down enough that the ponies only need swim a few strokes. (signed) The Wyoming Kid

Frank Comes to Wyoming 1918

Oshoto, Wyoming: Bob's brother, Francis (Frank), came by train from Sprague, Washington to Moorcroft, Wyoming. He came to help his Dad, Rarey Fir, with the improvements on the homesteads while Ferdie and Bob were in the Armed Services in France during World War I. Frank arrived in Moorcroft same time as Jess Driskill, of the D Ranch, came through with a trail herd of 500 head of longhorn cattle. Frank rode his Unicyle, a bicycle with only one wheel, and helped to trail those cows the first day, but on the second day he pulled out ahead of the herd as he could travel faster. When he came to a big yellow house, he stopped to ask how much further it was to Brislawns? "Why, it is just over those hills," answered Mrs. George Blatt, the neighbor adjoining their land, to the southwest. ---Mack and Dipper

Or There Wouldn't Be an Ireland

Bill McDonald was helping Rarey Fir with the homestead work while Ferdie and Bob were having all this fun in Texas and New Mexico. Rarey Fir wished them home as he missed them. Bob was concerned about the fact that Bill was doing such a good job his Dad wouldn't want him back! Bob was going to go over to Ireland to help with that uprising but his Dad told him he better save the World first from the Germans or there wouldn't be an Ireland. Bob thought that was right, so went to France. ---Nejl

France – World War I

"Cowards die a thousand deaths-- while Heros die only once." (Who said that?)

Bob Brislawn, John J. Binney, Clyde C. Hughes, James A. (Jim) Benson, Jim Madden and Harold P. Fawlkes were among the boys who all left together on a train...a girl came along passing out oranges, when Jim Benson was offered one, he said, " No, thanks, I didn't wear my slicker!"

They all left Wyoming together but were spit up and in different divisions of the armed forces while in France, except

Harold P. Fawlkes, he was with Bob Brislawn. Bob had it written in his Black Book: "In - May 20, 1918 Out - August 13, 1919" `My dog tag # C284845, "That was an easy one." Bob sent a post card marked "Soldiers' mail. No postage necessary", to his sister, Anastasisa Thomas of Yakima, Washington stating that "R. E. Brislawn had arrived safely overseas". Bob arrived in the harbor at Brest, France with American Expeditionary Forces under General John Pershing, and the Company C. 48th Engineers, Via New York. Bob said, "He carried his Knapsack up those steps many a time".

Brest Harbor

As Bob was with the Expeditionary Forces he was moved around to different locations to do whatever was necessary. They rebuilt bridges and railroad tracks behind the soldiers onthe front lines - within a day or two after the battles, to bring supplies to the front line soldiers. The troops that Bob was with were moved in railroad train boxcars...the kind livestock were hauled in. Bob said, "It was said, they could haul either 40 horses or 20 men in each boxcar."

Sometimes the enemy had moved back and would be hiding and waiting for them to come. Then the American Soldiers would have to charge out of that boxcar door running for cover while being picked off - shot one by one. Bob said that he never knew whether he would be the next one to die when he charged out that door and ran yelling and shooting while jumping over bodies of dead or dying Buddies.

Bob did this while carrying a knapsack on his back along with an axe and shovel to repair the railroad tracks or bridges. The knap-sack contained the food rations, and all his possessions and necessities such as ammunition. The rifle had a bayonet for hand-to-hand fighting. There were millions of refugees from the war-torn countries who were moving helplessly from place to place, seeking shelter in the ruins of bombed out buildings. Those who tried to return to their farms or homes often found that their villages no longer existed; the churches, schools, crops, factories, roads and railroads were all destroyed! Starvation, disease, and exposure caused hundreds of thousands of deaths. Spanish Influenza (disease warfare) caused millions of deaths. The people were dependent on the governments for food.

After the railroads and bridges were repaired the American Government sent in supplies, food and grain. The railroad boxcars of supplies were only reaching the select - then as now, the needs of the neediest were not met. The aid did not reach those who needed it the most. There would be large stockpiles of grain (Wheat) in the city's streets with sidewalks boarded off so grain would not run into the buildings, yet, the people in general could not use the grain - it all went to the governments, to be used politically or allotted out to certain people who used it for their own gain.

Seeing all the starving people and knowing that they were not allowed to get the grain from the stockpiles, Bob would switch a boxcar of wheat off onto a spur of the railroad track overnight so the people could come fill their washtubs or buckets, anything they had; the women would come and fill their aprons with the wheat to make flour to use to bake bread for themselves and their children.

When in Sprague, Washington during Bob's school days at Sprague Catholic School, the good nuns had taught him, starting in the first grade, to speak German and French. In the war, Bob would venture off into the night beyond the battle-grounds often into enemy territory to leave messages for the refugees... letting them know the whereabouts of the carload of wheat that would be left, a different boxcar at a different location every night; then in the morning he would get there early to switch the boxcar back on the regular track to be picked up and taken on to the Government stockpiles.

After several of these trips into the countryside the people learned Bob was there to help them

-- they gave him a password `Komrade'. Bob was good with codes and secret messages and since he could read, write and speak both German and French he could break the enemies secret codes... watch or listen for letters or numbers or certain words used often in a sentence; thus learned where the next enemy battles or air strikes would be made. When Bob received orders where he was to go on these secret trips into the countryside; "Message received and being carried out," was all Bob could report to his `Louie' at these times. Sometimes, Bob met the informant at the village or city Square. There was always a Square which was in a park like area at the center of the village with a monument of some hero. Often the monument was a statue of a hero on a horse; other villages at least had a monument or obelisk pillar of marble or granite sometimes with names engraved on it in memory of some hero or heroes. Sometimes they would meet at midnight or other time late at night or some other given time - usually they would meet before the curfew so they could blend in with the other people at the Square; if it was after dark, one of the signals used was, stand in the blackest shadows next to the monument/obelisk, roll a cigarette from the Bull Durham or Prince Albert Tobacco that he used then (later Bob quit smoking), take three puffs so the coals would glow in the dark, then throw the lighted cigarette out into the cobbled-stoned area... give the password then give the messages of where the carload of wheat would be that night - receive any messages of where the enemy was attacking and then Bob would drift off into the night - lost among the shadows.

The army headquarters where they were camped had guards walking their posts, keeping watch over the camp day and night, so Bob had to sneak in and out during the night; he would watch and listen for the guards to meet, greet each other with a pass word, turn and walk away, before he slipped across silently to go his way to make the contact and return... watch for footprints in the snow... don't make tracks... step in tracks or use well traveled trails... Great care had to be taken so that no one saw him hanging around certain places--if he saw his informant during the day he could not show signs of recognition--even a flicker of an eye could give the secret away...and the friends would be taken to prison or shot.

Battle of Verdun

When Bob told me that he "Was in the Battle of Verdun". I said, "That was in World War II."

Bob answered, "Well, there was a Battle of Verdun in World War I, cause I was there. It was like George Washington's Army in Valley Forge, they were surrounded by enemy all winter with the bitter cold and no supplies or reinforcements - they were being held down in this valley for days, the days turned into weeks, the weeks into months, besides the wounded and dead could not be cared for; the soldiers were freezing their feet and hands in the bitter severe cold - so they wrapped themselves in rags and blankets, whatever they could find to keep warm - there were many blood-soaked bandages.

The sniper fire held them down in the trenches or foxholes during the day so they could only move at night. Moving about during the cover of darkness to go help the wounded or the dying; eat their rations and prepare themselves for another day of battle.

During the day the Priests, Medics and Buddies were being killed when they tried to crawl under gunfire to help the wounded men. Medics would administer morphine or other drugs to the wounded or sick to keep them quiet... so they would not cry out in pain and draw the enemy gun-fire. Some of the wounded or sick soldiers refused the morphine and would lay quietly chewing on a piece of cloth or leather; only when they became delirious or unconscious were they given the morphine or drugs to keep them quiet, while others would cry out and beg for the morphine to ease their pain. Many soldiers came home addicted to the drugs.

The Priests crawled about the trenches and from foxhole to foxhole distributing the Sacraments of Holy Communion and when necessary, the Holy Oils and Absolution of the Last Rites to the sick and dying. Giving the men the grace of the Holy Spirit, trust in God, encouragement, comfort and strength to resist the anxiety about death, thus being able to bear their suffering bravely and also to fight against death.

Bob could see they were all being killed as slowly they were dying from exposure, disease or from the enemy gun-fire... that is when he decided that he might be able to use the password and get through the enemy line. Back in the States the Sioux Indians have a war cry 'huka hey' (HOH-kah-HAY) meaning a

`Good Day to Die', so following a hunch, Bob took the chance and made a run for it. `Hoka Hey`, he thought as he slipped away into the darkness, through the trees, through the enemy, giving the password of "Komrade". No one fired at him!

Bob made his way through the night until at daylight he saw an abandoned building that had been shelled and was partially fallen down... there he hid out. A beautiful young German girl found him and hid him in their cellar, attic, or barn and hayloft; moving him from place to place while the enemy soldiers were searching for him or other refugees. "She nursed me back to health just like in the movies or stories you read where the beautiful girl hides the hero in haylofts or cellars or some place... it was like that", Bob said.

Once Again Death Dashed Aside!

The World Book Encyclopedia states: "Germany tried to pierce the French line with a massive attack on Verdun. Crown Prince Frederick Wilhelm's Artillery shelled the city for 24 hours, on February 21, 1918. His troops attacked on a 20-mile front. A ring of defenses surrounded the city. General Heri Petain, commanding the French Second Army held off the Germans - the German troops advanced only about 4 miles in six months. They were within 4 miles of the city by June. Unable to advance further, the Germans went on the defensive. The French counterattacked. The French suffered more than 540,000 casualties, and the Germans lost more than 430,000 men."

Bob described how the prisoners were exchanged: They met on each side of a river bridge with the prisoner released on the enemy side by enemy officials to walk across the bridge to be met by Allied Officers. Like in the movie pictures and news reels.

Bob said, "I loved the rain, it made the plants grow and washed clean the air and earth; but the snow was 'more better' as it covered up the trash, filth and even the wounds of the battle fields; that the snow came and covered up the dead and the blood of the battle field giving the soldiers relief from the sights of war."

One Christmas during World War I, a 24 hour truce was called. Ferdie said the combat soldiers from both sides of the line laid down their guns and came into the no-man's land between the lines of trenches - built fires to keep warm, cooked and shared their rations - as friends - neither side as enemies. Then after the truce the soldiers from each side went back to their posts or positions and commenced firing - enemies again

Bob went to the people's house where the girl had befriended him to have Christmas Dinner with them; because there were other Americans there and German soldiers also, Bob couldn't let on he knew these people. nor could he let on he knew their languages. Once while dinner was being eaten he slipped with a word and got a puzzled look from a German, but nothing happened. It was the governments that were fighting. There was not the hate factor as there is now between the warring countries.

In some countries that are fighting now the children are taught from earliest childhood to hate certain people. Ferdie was in a trench when World War I ended...Ferdie said, "Could it have been the famous Eddie Rickenbacker (World War I, ACE) who flew over the trenches calling down, and dropping leaflets that the War was over?"

"The men from both sides of the line threw down their guns and ran to the no-man's land - this time to hug each other and dance around with shouts of joy."

Ferdie was discharged spring of 1919, he came home suffering from the poison gases and shell-shock, which remained with him the rest of his life. Bill McDonald was killed in France during World War I in the Argonne Forest. Bill was e Bob's buddy who went through school and graduated with him and who later came homesteading in Wyoming with Bob, Rarey Fir, and Ferdie. (The World Book Encyclopedia says that 1,200,000 Americans fought in the Battle of the Meuse- Argonne. One of every ten was killed or wounded.) Bob was at one of these secret meetings late at night standing in the shadows of an Onni or obelisk pillar type monument when he received the message that the War was over.

Bob slipped away back through the secret hideouts and trails of the `underground', along back to the front line and to the base-camp; but was picked up by the United States Army...and detained in the U. S. Army jail for 2 or 3 days. When Bob's Lieutenant learned of his whereabouts the `Louie' and some of Bob's Buddies came down and got him released. If they had not done this he would have been held as a Prisoner of War for sometime - .like a year or two?

After the War, Bob wrote to his `Louie' thanking him for the help. Nejl has the card that that `Louie' wrote back to Bob... it reads: "I know you appreciate it. It was all in a days work."

Bob must of been doing more than was asked of him as at the end of the War. Bob received a medal of commendation for Bravery in Service Above and Beyond the Call of Duty. Bob was `Over There' one year. When the War was over Bob and his buddie, Harold J. Fawkes, from Sundance, Wyoming, bummed their way through Europe and parts of Asia seeing all the sights. Bob arrived home from France in 1919 via the good ship the U.S.S. LEVIATHAN. In New York Harber -- Soldiers lining the deck. Hundreds of thousands of cheering people (including girl-friends and wives) met the ship at the DOCKS. Then a Ticker-tape parade was given for them down 5th Avenue of New York City. ALL WERE HEROS, on their return from the World War I.

Bob says, "Live your life in such a way (for the good) so you will be remembered after you are dead."

Years later, on Bob's death-bed, he worried about all the starving people all over the world. "When I close my eyes I can see them, like during World War I, when I was there", he said. World War I was called, `THE WAR TO END ALL WARS'. I write these things to condemn, not to glorify, war. ---Dipper

Horses in World War I

The late Charley Claar, of Moorcroft, Wyoming who had the drug store there for many years, told us that he was in the U. S. Cavalry during World War I, one of the mounted men who rode into battle. Charley Claar said they had a lot of different breeds of horses, some Thoroughbred or Thoroughbred crosses which often panicked under fire in the battle. Charley said that he would search the remount herd for the Spanish horse to ride as that was the one horse who wouldn't lose his head when the guns were blazing at them... the one who could pick his way through the barbed wire and would not panic when in a tight place but think his way out of it to safety... often saving Charley's life and other soldiers, as well. These Spanish Horses would charge the enemy; who could lose with help of the biting, gashing slashing teeth and with the two front feet pawing and the two hind feet kicking. ---Dipper

Section Six

Dipper tells about her Mom

starting with

The Irwins' Hard Times

Winter 1925: Erva Irwin and her daughters, Gennevieve and Fae, came by train from Holyoke, Colorado to Moorcroft, Wyoming. and then by Hugh Minnich's mailstage the 30 miles to Hulett, Wyoming. It was November or December so was very cold with snow covering the ground. The mailstage was a sled with a small building covering it, which was full of packages and bundles of mail so Erva and Gennevieve stood up inside but 7 year old Fae sat in the doorway with her legs dangling outside over the edge.

Hugh Minnich (Cash's Dad) stood outside in front of this cab so he could drive the team of horses. He froze his nose because he was outside. Usually Hugh could stand inside out of the cold while he drove the team with the reins through a window in the front, but this time there wasn't room for him in there too.

They came to Hulett to join their son and brother, Clifford. Clifford and wife, Luella, had come to Colony, Wyoming to work for Cola Shepard, who ran the Federal printing press there. He also had the

80

newspaper, The Colony Coyote News, that Clifford and Luella, printed while Cola himself worked at the Federal Press, printing forms for the government.

When Luella was 12 years old she had gone to work as a maid, for Erva in Emglewood Colorado, where she met Clifford. They were married when she was 14 years old. Three children were born of this union; Fae (Us Baby), and a son, Duane, born July 6, 1924, who was killed during World War II in Manila, Phillipines; and a son, William Freeman, born August 24, died September 30, 1927 of whooping cough and is buried in the Mount Moriah Cemetery near Sundance. Wyoming.

The July 2, 1925 issue of the Colony Coyote News was the last issue to be published by Clifford and Luella Irwin, who left the Colony community for Sundance, to publish a newspaper. However the Mayor and Judge in Sundance run Clifford out of town as they wanted him to go Republican but Clifford wanted to stay Independent. They moved to Hulett. They bought and brought their own printing press to Hulett. Also, they had newspapers in Brule and Paxton, Nebraska, so had three papers going at once.

July 23, 1925 The Crook County News started out. They also published Little Sentinel, an Independent Newspaper. Erva wrote and published in book form "Little Blue Pig"; a story of Little Blue Pig and what he found on Mt. Olympus.

May 11, 1926; Clifford D. Irwin was appointed United States Commissioner with office at Hulett, Wyoming. This from the newspaper, The Sundance Times, `Peek at the Past' column for May 29, 1986. He was 19 years old when Land Commissioner for Crook County, Wyoming, the youngest man to have held that office.

Erva's father's name was David Henry Freeman. He was a Clerk in the Army during the Civil War, and was with General Sherman in the march through the South. David Freeman belonged to the organization, Grand Army of the Republic. I have a medal ~In Memoriam', from HOLYOKE Post No. 51 G.A.R., Holyoke Colorado. David Freeman was in the real estate business there and was Justice of the Peace.

Erva Freeman was born in Juniata, Nebraska, April 9, 1881. Her mother died when she was born. Erva lived in Imperial, Nebr. When Erva was nine years old the family moved to Holyoke, Colorado, where she attended school and grew to womanhood.

When the Freemans lived in a mansion in Englewood, Colorado, at the top of a long hill, there was a street car running by pulled by a white horse. The horse would pull the street car up the hill, then get upon a platform on the back and ride down the hill.

When Erva was 18 years old she married Joseph Mack Irwin at Holyoke. to this union six children were born; Mabel, Clifford, Gennevieve, Russell, Cecil and Fae.

Joseph Mack Irwin was from Illinois; his mother's name was Sally Ann Tucker. They had come to Holyoke in 1890. In 1919 the family moved to Denver, Colorado where in 1924 her husband passed away. There had been a divorce, though, with the boys staying with their father Mack and the girls with Erva. Mack was good with horses and worked in a stable; Cecil stayed, even when the others married and moved on, to work in this stable with his father. It was here that Cecil met and knew Buffalo Bill Cody when he stabled his horse, Bridget, there. When Mack left there he took Cecil and went to Kansas.

Mabel married Freeman Finch in 1920. Then in a Model T Ford car they moved to California. They had six children, Gene, Keith, Lawrence, Oral, Ivan and Erva.

Russell married Velma, of Imperial, Nebraska, and Dean and Dorothy were born. Times were tough: both Velma and Luella left their husbands and children, leaving together on the same day for Denver. They were so young and times were so tough. Luella and Erva had to run the newspaper, The Crook County News. They had to get ads from Belle Fourche merchants and deliver the newspapers to New Haven and Sundance over dirt or gravel roads in those old high wheeled cars winter and summer. Luella said once she slipped off the icy road during a blizzard between Hulett and and New Haven. She had their two small children with her, so she took one in her arms and one by the hand to walk to the next ranch. After that she got to wondering and asking herself "Why am I doing this?"

Clifford had newspapers in Brule and Paxton, Nebraska where he worked part of the week, commuting to Hulett. `Us Baby' Fae remembers coming by train with her mother -- the train stopped out on the prairie at the signpost `KARA', between Upton and Moorcroft. It would be dark when they got off the train but some one was always there to meet them.

When Velma and Luella left, they put their children in an orphanage. Clifford finally found where his kids were, but had a hard time getting them out. Then he was told that there were some other kids there by the name of Irwin. When he looked he found to his surprise they were Dean and Dorothy, Russell's kids.

Erva said to Russell, "Come to Hulett and I'll help you take care of Dean and Dorothy". He did. "Us Baby" Fae and Duane were already there; Erva and Gennevieve took care of them. Fae helped too, but she was younger.

Russell said, "I didn't have a dime. Heard you could get work on the W.P.A. if you went over to Moorcroft to apply. Erva made over a man's suit to fit him. When the woman clerk saw him, she said, "Anyone dressed like that don't need this job." He did not get the job.

He wore his working clothes after that when applying for work and always got the job. I asked, what did you do then? Why, he said, Cecil and I broke 3 or 4 horses for $5 or $10 a horse. He used an old slick A-fork saddle that wasn't good for riding bucking horse. He rolled up a coat, tyed across the front, then he could ride them.

Clifford was instrumental in getting the Social Security Act passed. He went to jail in Denver, for marching in a demonstration.

Clifford married Lilyan Painter on February 17, 1934; they have two daughters, Stelina and Janice.

Gennevieve taught at the Little Missouri Buttes School. Pay was $80.00 per month. Out of that she had to pay for her board at Glasburn's. On weekends, Gennevieve rode horseback the 15 to 20 miles, back and forth between Hulett and Glasburn's. Often, Fae rode out there, too. Glasburns didn't have children of their own so took them in and treated them as their own.

In those days anyone who graduated from high school could teach school. Gennevieve got her teaching degree while living in Hulett and teaching school. Gennevieve attended the University of Wyoming at Laramie and Normal School in Spearfish, South Dakota. ---Dipper

Crook County, Wyoming

Popular Oshoto Couple Married Here Saturday

(From a newspaper clipping)

"Robert Brislawn of Oshoto and Miss Gennevieve Irwin of Hulett were united in marriage at the Catholic Church here Saturday

morning, April 9th. Rev. Fr. Schneiders of Newcastle officiating, the ceremony being attended by a few friends of the couple.

The bride is the daughter of Mrs. Erva Irwin, publisher of the Crook County News at Hulett and is one of the popular school teachers in the Oshoto community. The groom is a progressive young rancher of near Oshoto."

NOTE: Bob and Gennevieve were married in Upton, Wyoming, at Saint Antoney's Catholic Church, April 9, 1931. Bob had to leave almost immediately for Colorado, to work on the survey. Bob said, it was the hardest thing he ever had to do. ---Dipper

In the Flutter of Angles' Wings

May 4, 1943, Oshoto, Wyoming: Mama and her dying. For a week she lay dying; refusing to go see the Doctor as she thought she was having the flu, or female troubles as didn't know what it was - but finally Dad insisted she go and loaded her up and took her in to Dr. Clarenbaugh in Sundance on May 4, 1943.

Mama was 34 years old; her birthday. Mama had been refusing to go, saying "If I go, I know I am not coming back." Finally she consented to go - .Bob helped her out to the Tarraplane car and laid her on the back seat where Mildred Sherwood, our school teacher, had put blankets for a bed with pillows at one end for Mama to lay on.

Bob and Mildred went back into the house after something when Mama called me to her as she lay in the back seat - all pale and sickly looking. Mama said,"she had something to tell me that she didn't want Emmett to hear". Since Emmett and I had an blood-pact agreement to know everything about each other but never tell, he got to come, too. I knelt down in the front seat looking back at Mama, when she said: "she only wanted me there, needed to tell me something." Then she asked me, "To take care of the others as she wasn't coming back."

Neil went with Dad and Mama to the doctor, to help care for Mama in the car, while three year old Colleen and nine-month old Shane were left in my care that day as Mildred Sherwood was working around the house. Emmett, 11 years old, had to saddle up Tyee to ride to check on a cow who was calving. Emmett couldn't pull the calf so he went for Uncle Frank to come help. Uncle Frank came and he couldn't pull it. So they went to Oshoto to phone the Veterinary. The vet came and he couldn't pull it either, so they ended up putting Uncle Frank's jeep on the chains and pulled the calf. It was dead. The cow lived a few days, then died.

Before Bob left he said he would come back through the hills by the big windmill if things were or went bad at the doctors - if everything going to be all right he would come home by the D Road and then later go up to turn the windmill off so the water tank would not run over. Later that afternoon, I was pushing Colleen and Shane on the homemade swing-set that was still over by the Homestead Shack when I saw the Tarraplane car with Bob driving coming over the ridge above Grand Dad's Orchard. I knew things were bad by that signal so started to take Colleen and Shane to the house. I had not gone far was just starting to cross that little draw between the Homestead Shack and the New House when I heard the flutter of Angel's wings.

I felt someone put their arm around my shoulders in a hug, their arm was across my back and shoulders, when I heard someone tell me, "Your mother is dead". I felt that one Angel, but saw 7 others standing around beside me towards the back - there was one Angel at my back that I could not see, none out in front. I could hear the flutter of their wings. Shane had a hold of one of my hands so he could walk while Colleen had a hold of his other hand as she toddled along, as Bob drove up by the New House.

When Bob got out of the car he held his arms out to us all, then picked up Colleen and Shane - then he looked at me and said, "Your Mama is dead".

I said, "I know", as I ran to the car, expecting to see Mama still in the back seat, but, of course, she wasn't. Bob had stayed at the hospital, a two story building on the main street entering Ssundance, for about two hours. Gennevieve was feeling much better and seemed most likely to be fine. They decided he could go on home and come back for her in a couple days. She had brought personal items and books to read. Bob and Neil then started to the telephone office before heading for home. As they approached the telephone office, the operator rushed out, waving her arms and franticly shouting, "Get back to the hospital as fast as you can.

Your wife is dieing."

Bob turned the car around in the street, running over the sidewalk and somebody's lawn.

Mama died about an hour later.

Neil told me later, "That he knew she was dead but never seemed to think what all that would amount to in our lives".

The emptiness and the tears of not having Mama there to take care of us and not being there to do things for us as we grew up. Not having her loving care. Bob went to the Telephone Office that was then in the house behind the old Sundance Bank. Ruby Sager was working as Telephone operator at the time and was heart-broken along with Bob as she helped him place the phone calls. Ruby Sager told me later, "Neil was playing around on the floor and didn't seem to understand what had happened...."

Neil would be 5 years old in 3 weeks. It rained for 2 weeks, making the dirt roads impassable, so Mama's body was kept in Sundance by the Undertaker. There was an abandoned jail - a jail from the earliest days of settling the town of Sundance in a basement under a grocery store on the corner, a building adjacent to the Higbee's Cafe, it was the old Elkhorn Cafe which is across the street west of the Courthouse Square. You can still see the rockwork walls and barred windows from the ally. I can see in my mind - the casket sitting in that jail cell on the floor or a bunkbed - with the rain pouring down heavy against the barred windows. Mama's body was kept in there where it would be cool until the roads dried enough so someone could get to Sundance.

Harry Berger had a 4 wheel drive, jeep station wagon so

he went for the body. Del Evens went with him. They met us all at the Pine Grove Cemetery. The Pallbearers had to carry the casket by hand across that boggy creek crossing below the reservoir there, to the old school house that was used for the funeral service. Mama's forehead was cold, when I kissed her good-by. Then they carried the casket on to the grave. The sun was shining that day -- but not for us. ---Dipper

The Legacy of Gennevieve Mae Irwin Brislawn

Gennevieve Mae Iwrin Brislawn (1909-1943) Born May 4, 1909 to Joseph Mack and Irva Freeman Irwin in Holyoke, Colorado. So much has been said about "Only the good die young." What was the woman like behind the man of Bob Brislawn?

Or maybe it was the LOSS of the woman behind the man. There is so much about Gennevieve but here are a few of her characteristics and ideals: She kept a six by eight black three ring loose leaf note book with her budgets (she always had a few dollars left over); the addresses of her friends and relatives; her collection of poems, some she wrote herself. We called this "The Black Book"

Bob kept his records and a diary of sorts in this Black Book after his wife, Gennevieve, died. Gennevieve played the

Violin. Her favorite song was "Happy Times are Here Again." I remember her singing "When its Spring Time in the Rockies" I'll be coming home to you." We were waiting for our Dad, Bob, to return from one of his many surveying trips away from home. They loved each other very much and missed each other. Uncle Frank and Aunt Fae both told me that Bob and Gennevieve both sang this song, both thinking about the other, as Bob sang it when he was away.

Another song Gennevieve sang was called "The Great Speckled Bird". In Gennevieve's Black Book, I found a list of 75 rpm phono- graph records, of the songs she liked: 1). Door of My Dreams/ Indian Love Call; 2). Spring Song / Minuet; 3). By The Weeping Waters / By the Waters of Minnetonka; 4). Anvil Chorus / Royal Italian March; 5). Beautiful Isle of Somewhere/Rock of Ages; 6). Love's Old Sweet Song/Gypsy Love Song; 7). Two Black Crows, Part I/Part II; 8). Two Black Crows, Part III/Part IV; 9). Some- where A Voice is Calling / Whispering Hope; 10). Humoreske/ Berceuse; 11). My Wild Irish Rose / I Love the Name of Mary; 12). Barcarolle (Badly cracked)/ Melody in F.; 13). Silent Night, Holy Night / Adeste Fideles; 14). There's A Rainbow Round My Shoulders/Sonny Boy; 15). Whistler and His Dog/Warblers Serenade; 16). Narcissus / To a Wild Rose--To A Water Lily; 17). It Goes Like This/Rhythm King.

Gennevieve lived by `The Golden Rule' of do unto others as you want them to do onto you. Gennevieve was not just a Sunday Christian, as we went to church on Sundays when we could, even with a team and wagon in the summer then the team and sled in the winter, 3 miles each way to Carl and Maggie Blatt's; or 5 or 6 miles to Pete and Margaret Svalina's; or our place, when the priest came once a month from Newcastle, Wyoming 90 miles away to the Mass which was held in our homes.

But the whole out-of-doors was her Cathedral. Gennevieve was planning on being Baptized into the Catholic Church, on the last time we went to church about two weeks before she died, but something happened that the priest didn't. I don't know why or what went wrong. Later priests have told me that Gennevieve had "The Baptism of Desire." So went to Heaven, I know she did.

Gennevieve was very cheerful and always saying nice encouraging things to people. Making them feel better about themselves. She was fun to be around but mostly she cared and was concerned about the others. Gennevieve was 5 feet 4 inches tall, with straight black hair and brown eyes. Bob called Gennevieve, "Gene" or "Love". Gennevieve was quite an artist, but her favorite was drawing caricatures of mice all dressed up as people.

They raised chickens, pigs and turkeys for food. Gennevieve baked the bread, and done the cooking. Food was hard to come by after she died. Gennevieve made a lot of our clothes. she made Colleen's and my dresses from the flour sack material. We picked out the color and print of the dress we wanted when they brought the sack of flour, and we had some cute dresses. I have a denium skirt and vest she made for me. She always kept us clean. Most all of Gennevieve's clothes are gone; except a remnant of her coat of many colors, like Joseph's coat in the bible. Later Bob had a neighbor, Hazel Turnquist, make it into a vest for himself. The Vest is now on display in the Crook County Museum. Sundance, Wyoming. Mama was nicknamed, "Nimbleheels", because she could dance. She could still kick the top of the door frame at age 33, before she died. She was a Ballerina; taught Ballet and Tap Dancing; danced the Charleston, could dance them all.

When Fae was in high school, Gennevieve and Fae were going to put on an exhibition after some school program. Gennevieve to do an Egyptian Dance. Fae was to do a Spanish Dance. Grandma, Erva, made the costumes all so authentic, with the Egyptian skirt slit up the sides. They practiced for weeks. Everything had to be just so with their hand movements -- clothes and all authentic. Then when the Superintendent or Principal, whoever it was, came out on stage to give the introduction, he said, that he nor the school would take responsibility for the next exhibit. It was all very insulting. So Gennevieve got mad, pulled and broke off all the layers of beads, beads flew everywhere.........neither Gennevieve nor Fae went on stage that night. So insulted. Nothing wrong..... except in those days, the slits up the sides of the skirt on both sides were open to Gennevieve's hips, showing her legs. The times were then that that was unheard of.....as women didn't even wear slacks or jeans in those days! Fae was dressed in a Spanish costume so it was okay - but she didn't go on stage either! * * * * * * * *

When Fae graduated from high school everyone was so poor. Times were tough for everyone all over the country. No one had money to buy her a dress to wear to the graduation. Bob and Gennevieve sent Fae $50.00 to buy a dress. Fae said she will never forget that.

On these survey expeditions we were camped out, lived in tents, cooked on campfires; used horses, did have vehicles to go from place to place but trailed the horses most of the time. It's been said, "that if a person's heart is in the right place, it doesn't matter whether one lives in a shack or in a mansion - they will be happy wherever they are". Bob said, that "Mama was content and happy just as long as she had us kids, and him, whether we were living in a tent; or the homestead shack. or the new house."

Gennevieve didn't need to be entertained. She loved living in the country. Gennevieve quoted a saying: "Some people feel the rain, while some people just get wet." When asked why he never re-married, Bob would say, "that Gennevieve was the perfect wife, so unselfish, so he would not take the chance of re-marrying." "That he didn't want to chance having a wicked-step-mother for us."

Bob had three proposals that I know of, as at different times a year or two after Gennevieve died, there were three woman who called me into the kitchen and told me that they wanted me to hear this, as they asked Bob to marry them.

Colleen says the only time she can remember Mama was

the time there was a grass fire across the draw, when Rarey Fir's barn burnt down. It burnt 15 to 20 acres of grassland over the hill and ridge south west of the draw. Mama was across the draw along the fence of the two acre pigpen and three year old Colleen wanted to go over there with Mama, but they wouldn't let her go, so Colleen stood there by the end of the row of cottonwood trees and cried and cried and looked at Mama over there. Mama had been washing clothes. Since she heated the water on the wood range/stove she usually baked Bread the same day she washed clothes to make use of the heat from the fire. I was left in charge of finishing the bread baking; and the clothes washing; while watching Colleen.

Mama always made a home with tender loving care, wherever we were. A few times I saw her cry: Once when Dad lost his wallet and then when she became lost in the big cities, like Salt Lake City. Mama drove one car while Dad drove the other to and from wherever Dad was working and the Cayuse Ranch. Mama would be following Dad and the street light changed, cutting us off from Dad. Then other cars and trucks might get in between us so we couldn't see which direction Dad turned. Mama would pull off to the side of the road to wait until Dad came back to find us. Once we had to go to the closest Police Station and officers there would help us find Dad or he would come there to look for us. That is what he told us to do, go there to wait for him to come.

A collection of poems that Gennevieve had in her Black Book: Some of the poems were: "Limpy" about 'There's an empty bunk in the bunkhouse tonight". There sure was an emptyness at our house after Mama died. A poem of "The Cowboys Prayer', about loving the wild wide open country; One poem was, "When the bloom is is on the sage, I want to be in Texas, just a riding on the range." One poem was about an old woman, who guarded the flag during the Civil War when the rebel soldiers in Ferderigtown, hauled down the flag, she grasped it up and kept it, saying, "Shoot if you must this old gray head, but leave alone the flag. Another was about Guardian Angels, there must be or else how could little boys grow to be a man. Some of the poems she wrote are:

Just Keep On

Just keep on a livin' And keep on a givin'. And keep on a trying to smile, Just keep on a singin'. And trustin' an' a clingin' to the promise of an after awhile. For the sun goes up and the sun goes down, And the morning follows night. Where a place to rest, Like a mother's breast. An' a time when things come right. Just keep on believin' An' a hidin' all your grievin', And keep on a tryin' to cheer, Just keep on a prayin' A lovin' and a' saying', The things that we love to hear. For the tide goes in an' the the tide goes out, And the dark will all turn bright, There's a rest from the load, And an end to the road, An' a place where things come right.

"Life and Love and a bright sky o'er us, And--God take care of the way before us."

* * * * * I remember that sometimes the front door of our new

house would be opened as if someone turned the door-knob and came in, then closing the door behind them, but no one there - when this happened, although we didn't see any one, Gennevieve would laugh and say, "Come in, Come in, whoever you are." It was just matter-of-fact and not scary at all. Then there was another poem of Gennevieve's belief:

That the Dead return. I know they do to linger close and share the joys and grief that came, as in bygone days. That all we are, the dead can see, All Things about us here they know, and tho, we never see them here, their spirits hover very near. The dear father and sweet mother come back to hover close to their sons and daughters to protect and guide. * * * *

Gennevieve left us a word of hope with this poem:

There's a Road Beyond Tomorrow Where the Skies are blue again, There is hope to follow sorrow. Just as sunshine follows rain. And, Altho' the rain is falling And the skies are gray, not blue, On the Road Beyond Tomorrow There are brighter days for you."

An obituary leaves so much un-said: It don't tell of the love, concern, or care this person done for her family, or what she meant to us, or the things left un-done from then on. ---Dipper

Section Seven

Family Survey Travel – Far Distant Places

Before There Was Any Family

Bob and I (Frank wrote) worked with Steward Penick for the United States Geological Survey, Marble Colorado; 1926 or 1927, South and East of Glenwood Springs. At the end of work in October we went to Salt Lake by train and bought a Model T for thirty-five dollars. It was open, only a windshield. No paved roads, dirt or corragated gravel. the tires inflated to 60 pounds, sure rough. Stopped at Baker, Oregon to visit Marian vent Kligel, our neice, and on to Umatilla, Oregon. Crossed the Columbia on a boat to Plymouth, Washington. 100 miles or more around by Pasco and only 30 across the Horse Heaven Country, so we went. Just one sand dune after another. Broke a spring and hobbled into Praser. "The land was put into wheat during W. W. I and it was only sand, and one crop." Up to Yakima to visit our sister, Tat and family, then on to Spraque to our sister, Alice, and her son, Jimmy.

Then on to Spokane to visit some more relations, Claud Brislawn who was unhappily married to Mamie Kennedy. For one thing no one could stay over with them, so we agreed to test her out. She was ashamed of her environment. We said, we'd go. But she begged us to stay, so we did. The next day was lovely so Claud said, "You better stay over its so lovely". But Mamie said, "Its a good day to travel". So we did.

Well, after a day or so we got to Crow Agency, Montana. It was dark so we went a little east and threw our beds down. Awoke at sun-up. There were Indian girls all around, laughing. They had buckets and were on their way to get water from the river. Our pants were over by the car, so the girls tee hee'd.

The old Model T was bucking and had it looked at in Sheridan, but could find nothing. It was bum gas. Shooked and bounced over the graveled wash board road to Gillette, got some eats and gas, then drove out of town a half mile, it was dark so unrolled our beds at what looked like a homestead, a hole dug 10 X 4 for a cellar. At daylight we sat up and looked around. Tombstones all around! We were in the cemetery! Made it on home that day.   ---Frank

Colorado 1929; Red Mountains, Gore Range. The Gore is the most rugged and broken of all the Rocky Mountains system. Big snow 1st of September. ---Bob

Colorado 1931: Climbed Powell Peak and found a can in a cairn with his name and names of his party in the can. He as I remember was there in 1873. So we took the honor to put our names in the can. Hope some Forest Ranger sees this. On the back of an envelope Bob wrote the list of names that were in that cairn. (The envelope was found in among Bob's 80 years gathering.):

Powell Elev. 13524 Camp Lake Elev. 12267 Trip made August 23, 1873 Major J. W. Powell Tom Bancroft F. T. Sardmen F. V. Hayden M. D. Whitney

Now the Family - Emmett and Dipper Born

Emmett born 1932 September 11th. Dipper born March 24, 1934 Both Emmett and Dipper were born in the Homestead shack with only neighbor women as mid-wives. No doctors were there. A doctor from Moorcroft, Wy., came out in a few days to issue the Birth Certificates. The cost $35.00. (On my Birth Certificate it shows B. W. Earle, Moorcroft, Wyoming.) I was named Mabel after my Aunt Mabel, and Gennevieve after my mother, but I was soon nicknamed Dipper by Emmett who was just learning to talk, when they tried to have him call me, "Sister", he would say, "Dipper". ---Dipper

Erva Irwin, Died, May 9, 1935

Erva Freeman Irwin passed from this life at at her home in Hulett, Wyoming. She had been in poor health for several years and late Wednesday night had a sudden heart attack, while cooking supper, she fell over on to the hot stove. Doctor Bostwick was summoned but the attack proved fatal. Gennevieve held her family together after Erva died. ---Dipper

Mapping the Tetons

"May 1935: Robert E. Brislawn and family leaving to spend the next several months in the Tetons; where Bob will be mapping those mountains." (Item in The Crook County News.) Bob told us that he was one of the first to climb many of the highest peaks in Rocky Mountain Ranges. In a mountain climbers' guide to the Teton Range in Wyoming says that "T. F. Murphy was Chief of Party assigned by the U. S. Geological Survey in the early 1930's to map Grand Teton National Park. Murphy and his two assistants - Mike Yokel, Jr., and Robert E. Brislawn - are recorded as being the probable first climbers of a number of major peaks in the Tetons in the years 1933 to 1936." ---Dipper

Yellow Jacket

Lander, Wyoming 1937: You remember Yellow Jacket, he was a feral horse caught by the Indians out of the St. Lawrence Basin, Wyoming. Snow got awfully deep in the Basin so these ponies get out on the bunch grass hills above Sage Creek and in with some domesticated Indian Ponies. The Indians got around the bunch so they couldn't break for the timbered basin, and tryed to chase them down to a corral in the valley. Yellow Jacket broke from the bunch, tryed to escape by jumping a dry wash 20 feet deep and 40 feet across. He landed in the bottom with five young bucks on top of him. They tied him down and as it was getting dark left him there until morning, the rope tied around his belly and his feet to this. That is why Yellow Jacket had that big hole in his side. Took Yellow Jacket to camp. He was still wild. Put hobbles on him, tied his head to his bobbles and turned him loose with the others. When the ponies came in every morning for that cup of oats, I just put his out in a washbasin, but he wouldn't eat it so I had to catch him and put a nose bag on him with a little of the best grass mixed with the oats to get him started. He soon was one of the Bunch and the Chief's pet horse on the bad hard trails. Yellow Jacket was hit by lightning near a rocky pinacle on the ranch. This pinacle is also yellow so is now called Yellow Jacket along with the draw that runs by it. ---Bob

Nejl Born

Nejl born May 29, 1937. Nejl was born in a hospital in Lander, Wyoming. Bob could remember Nejl's birthday because it was the same year he got the horse, Yellow Jacket. ---Dipper

The Grand Teton National Park

We went back and forth a lot of different years, between Grand Teton National Park, Pinedale, Daniel, Big Sandy and the ranch home near Oshoto. Sometimes the horses were trucked over there in the spring of the year and then back in the fall, by Ray Bellows and Cecil Irwin, and Bob. Twice the horses were trailed back home. We were already home, when Ray Bellows or someone came by to get Cecil, to go with him to the Teton's to trail the horses back. Cecil went without his coat! It was warm when he left! He borrowed a coat, from Bob, as it turned cold. That was when Floyd Bellows came, Bob needed help on this survey so Bob went to the woods near Hulett, Wyoming where Floyd was cutting trees. Bob took the axe out of Floyd's hands, and Floyd went to work on the survey. Floyd went on to be a big man in the surveying business. ---Dipper

The Trail Home from the Tetons

To Oshoto, Wyoming: "One year the Survey crew was late getting though mapping in the Teton Area. Some horses pulled out for home before a bad storm. So we stayed late hoping to find those five horses, just about waited until too late getting out of the mountains, but got out before the storm hit," Bob wrote.

Jim Ross and Bob were trailing the horse-herd. Some of the horses carried panniers with our camp supplies. Uncle Cecil, Mama's brother, was driving our car, the Durant. with Mama, Emmett, Nejl and I. We were following along behind.

While coming down though the mountain area the road was more of a wagon-trail than a road. We went on until came to a dry ravine with 15 to 20 feet deep steep banks, there was a bridge of sorts, only the posts were set solid with planks nailed to them with unpeeled logs laid loosely cross-ways for the flooring of the bridge; with a lot of space between the logs so they could roll over or slide apart; Bob, who was the one driving on that day, would not drive across this rickety bridge; we couldn't go around; we couldn't fix the bridge; it would take too long a time and we couldn't go back.

Cecil decided he could drive the car across, which he did, very slowly; easing the car-tires over those loose poles. Mama, Emmett, Nejl and I walked down though the ravine and back up the other side. We watched as our Uncle Cecil drove slowly across, inch by inch! Of course, the horses had no trouble getting across.

Coming over Togwatee Pass, (Elevation 9,658 feet) the Durant would only go so far before it would quit, stall out. Emmett would have to jump out quickly to put a short log or fence post behind the wheel to keep the car from rolling back down the hill or mountain. Then we would wait a little while and the Durant would go a ways further. They backed up some of the steepest longest hills.

On the way though the Shoshoni Desert a black horse of Driskill's went to the wild bunch. Jim Ross, riding Ole Brownie, went out and got him back. Jim rode up into the herd of wild

103

horses and roped the black horse out of the herd of fast running horses.

The snow storm hit us in the Shoshoni area. It was a blizzard with high winds and 3 feet of snow. Bob, Mama and us kids, slept in the car. Cecil and Jim each had to un-roll their bed-rolls outside on the ground. Next morning or whenever the storm was over, we looked to see where they were. It looked flat out across there as there wasn't even a mound in the snow to show where Cecil was. Jim had kept an air-hole open in the snow where he was. We were concerned that Cecil might of smothered under all that snow. Bob hollared and Cecil sat up and came out of the snow. Then Jim crawled out of the snow and his bed, also. No one was even frost-bitten.

There was a fenceline near by, Bob kicked around in the snow and found an old fence post, and got a fire going. In that Shoshoni Desert country, a jack-rabbit has to carry his lunch. If you think it is bleak when you drive though in your easy-chair car, you ought to see it in a blizzard. Jim Ross, no stranger to the harsh cold of the Wyoming winters and snow storms, who knew how to survive the cold, later told his son-in-law, Mike Habeck, that he "Just about didn't make it," When he was talking about this blizzard.

Route taken was through Togwatee Pass, Dubois, then cross country to Thermopolis, on through the Hole in the Wall and Keycee, on to the Pumpkin Buttes and then Gillette. On out Highway 59, to Weston, then Eest on a county road to the Cayuse Ranch on the D Road. North of Pumpkin Buttes it was decided that we could go on home, leaving Jim to bring the horses.

It was a fenced highway lane all the way so one person could bring/trail the horses without trouble. Jim Ross would bring them on to his homestead North of Gillette on Little Powder River and then on to our home. I remember Jim leaning over looking into the drivers side window of the Durant, telling Bob, "If I'm not at your place in 5 days, come looking for me."

Fifth day came and Bob kept watching the road for Jim, watching the horizon 3 or 4 miles away - towards the L. A. Brown Ranch. Then decided to load us in the car and head out. Got as far as the L. A. Brown Ranch talking with Buster and Patsye Brown when Ed and Anna Norfolk came; it seems Ed had saw Jim and was bringing the message over as far as Browns, who could then take it on over to us, but we were there. No telephones so Jim had sent the message that he was laying over a few days at his home on Little Powder River before coming on with the horses. Jim had stayed at the Gillette Bars too long. Tim, Runt, Paint and Brownie were among the 20 or 30 head of horses trailed home; some were Driskill horses from the D Ranch. ---.By Bob and Dipper

Return to the Tetons

The next spring we returned to the Tetons for Bob to work on the survey. They found three of the five lost horses. Bob found Yellow Jacket, Tyee and Pony, where they had wintered on willowbark in a basin called the Devils' Kitchen. The horses had eaten the willow trees right down to the stubs.

Pony: In previous years, on his home-range on the Cayuse Ranch, Cecil had roped too many big ones on him and it ruined his kidneys. Pony was Cecil's horse. Pony was struck by lightening on the ridge south of Uncle Frank's on Uncle Ferdie's old homestead; Lightening; does strike twice in the same spot as many years later Dad had another gentle horse, named Muggin's, who was killed when he was struck by lightening along with three yearling colts who were hit by the lightening at the same time, on that same ridge and location as Pony. Yellow Jacket, also, was struck by lightening,and killed, further south in that same pasture but close by where Uncle Ferdie's buildings used to be. That draw is named after Yellow Jacket. By Dipper

On Good Going

Just wrote a note about the old Chief, Murphy. I packed for him in the Wind River Range. Made me think of the time they pulled a fast one on Frank Williams.

When the rodman quit to go to school, Mr. Murphy hired Frank. Frank had been riding for the Wind River Cattle Association. Had his own horse, a good grey, 1150 pounds, and we didn't have to prove it, Frank admitted his horse was the best. At least he was the biggest horse in camp.

So the Chief says to the Recorder, "lets see as how fast this horse is against these Indian Ponies in rough country. Bogs, logs, and rocks."

So at quitting time, seven miles from camp, the Chief say, "Frank, give me a shot at the turn of the trail. Mark the spot and come back, we will quit for today."

So he waved Frank down and put up the plane table, this being putting the instrument, tripod, and plane table on old Paint. Turned Paint loose to follow and high tailed it for camp. Got in, unpacked and unsaddled, gave the ponies a little grain. The ponies eat and I took off their nosebags. They rolled and went off to graze, and then here came Frank. The Chief say, "We were just beginning to worry about you, Frank"

"You didn't need worry, I would have caught you if I had any good going"

"That's right," the Chief says, "just too rough going for a big horse. It's like the cavalry chasing Indians".

They had Tyee, Chester, and Old Paint. Frank is still looking for smooth going so to get even on those ponies. I moved camp over the old Indian trails, 15 miles, while the other party, good horses, had to go around, 45 miles. But on good going these Indian ponies couldn't travel with those big pack horses. by Bob

Chopo

"What is the toughest horse I ever rode? Well, I have had a few good ones. A horse don't need to be good today, so he isn't. Well, rein your Quarter Horses close by and I will say this: Chopo

107

and Hoot were 2 of the best. Hoot out of Kentucky Whip (same was the old Quarter Horse breeding - Spanish and racing Thoroughbred).

Chopo a chunky little bay 900# mustang out of stock brought to Moorcroft by the 101 Ranch. (Topsye S.M.R. #34, same stock.) Chopo would trot 10 miles every hour forever - or at least where you were going. Always came out from Moorcroft in 3 hours. (30 miles.) Hoot was good but more beautiful. Chopo would make Hoot stretch his neck to keep up. I ended up loosing them both. Had them in the Tetons and when it got to looking like winter those 2 ponies hit for home. Never found them but heard they got as far as Casper.

Hoot was 15 hands 1050# and I guess would bring home a ribbon for beauty. For I was riding him for the mail in the Tetons. Just got to a ranch where they were branding as the Foreman rode up to the mail box on the road. The mailman had left a small box of groceries. The Foreman took a look at Hoot and then another look and said, "Great horse. I would sure like to show him to those waddies there at corral. Are you in a sweat?"

"No", I said, "I just like to be at camp when the Chief gets in - as he will be anxious for the mail."

So I goes down and branding stops. Those cowhands picked up his feet and took my saddle off to look see his withers - today they look at a horses rear, same as they look over a Bull." Signed: "The Wyoming Kid"

Bob's Gentle Outlaw

A neighbor, Mickey Pollack, came walking in to Rarey Fir's homestead, as he needed to borrow a horse to ride the remaining five miles to his home. Only horse there was Bob's old gentle outlaw, Chopo. Mickey got on and Chopo bucks over to the draw. When Chopo headed down the draw Mickey steps off, good thing he did as Chopo bucked underneath a tree ripping off two branches and stripped the bark off another with the saddle horn when he bucked over the hand-dug well.

Mickey walked home after all that. It was a short time after this that Frank had to go over to Ed Pollacks to bring home a set of harness and so Bob set Frank on Chopo. it must of been alright with Chopo because Bob said so. Frank spent the night, next morning 16 year old Perry Wells saddled up Chopo to run the other horses in. Chopo bucked all over the flat, really snapping and popping Perry's head and neck; but he rode him; until Chopo quit bucking, then went on to chase the horses in with him.

Then they put the harness on Chopo so it was hanging over the saddle and flopping and dangling down around Chopo's legs and flanks. Frank climbed on, first pulling Chopo's head around and stepped on from the front. Then headed for Bob's. Frank said he was scared to death, but Chopo never bucked with him. They made it back to Bob's...getting on and off through five gates, but no trouble. Back at Bob's barn, Frank gave Chopo a feed of oats and petted him, telling him what a swell boy he was, then took the harness and saddle off.

Chopo and Pancho

Chopo was out of Arizona Spanish Mustang stock brought to Wyoming 1908 by the 101 Ranch of Moorcroft. -- Bob.

Bob wrote he got Pancho from a Columbus and Dorto Cowboy in New Mexico. Pancho and Chopo were identical bay geldings, both outlawed one-man horses of Bob's. Frank told me June 27th, 1980, "he could tell which one was Chopo as Chopo had an injury which left a piece of flesh and skin hanging down hrom his hip, it was caused by a coyote bite when he was a day or so old." Bob had a song he sang about Chopo: I don't know who wrote it but Bob had it written on an inside cover of an empty stationary tablet where I found it in 1981: "Chopo, My cowhorse Chopo, my pride Across the vast mountains and prairies so wide, Across the swift rivers on Chopo, I ride. My Little Chopo -- from the Animus town across Texas Alamo to the Salt River Pegas I rode you, Chopo. Chopo Amigo Chopo my pride from the Mexico Border, cross Texas Alamo to the Salt River Pegas I rode you, Chopo."

Bob told me, "how true it was as he rode Chopo and Pancho all over Texas."

Emmett told of a time when Bob and him were at `old

lady Nick's'. Chopo bucked, but quit after bucking Bob's hat off. Bob got off to get his hat, got back on and the same thing happened. The second time Bob rolled up his hat and tied it with the saddle strings to his saddle. That was okay with Chopo so they rode the twenty miles on home without any more bucking.

Another time, Bob got on Chopo by the barn, Chopo bucked up by the Homestead Shack and back to the salt blocks. Bob said, "Chopo if you don't quit bucking I'm going to fall off". Chopo quit bucking. Bob and Chopo had something between them with Chopo bucking the way he did as Chopo quit bucking when Bob told him too. --- Dipper

Chopo, Hoot, Brownie, Tyee, Tim, and Paint

'Hoot' was the horse I learned to ride on. Bob called Hoot a `ladies horse' maybe because Mama and I rode him and maybe because he was beautiful! Hoot was solid black with the exception of one white sock on the off hindfoot. The hoof was black. His ears were tipped so that they nearly touched at the tip.

Frank says, "he helped Bob with Hoot's schooling and named him Hoot because he looked like an owl!"

Using Hoot on the survey, Bob would put the pack saddle on Hoot and `throw' the diamond hitch around the pack; supplies on each side; bedrolls on top with a place right in between the bedrolls where he put me, from the time I was able to sit up - he'd put me on, saying You're' safe there, no way I could fall off."

Hoot's lead rope was either tied up to the pack or removed

so that he was turned loose to follow in the pack-string. The same with my brother, Emmett, on Brownie. The earliest I can remember was of Hoot in the pack-string, climbing mountains and swimming rivers with me safe on his back. "I cut my teeth on a pack-saddle not the saddle-horn."

Bob worked his way through the Teton's and the Wind River Range. Me on Hoot and Emmett on Brownie. Once when Bob was setting a Bench Mark, Brownie was hanging around loose with Emmett on the pack when Brownie was spooked by a brown bear, Brownie ran for camp. When Bob got back to camp, about an hour later, there was Brownie grazing while Emmett was sound asleep on his back.

Once when moving camp the river was deeper than they expected so the horses had to swim. The sacks of flour, their three months supply, that were on the packs was wet and thought ruined. Their flour was an important part of their groceries and couldn't get any more until they finished the survey in that area. Bob and Uncle Frank said, not to be too hasty in throwing the flour away, as the water might of soaked in about an inch or so. It had, the rest of the flour was usable, as the water in the lakes, creeks, streams and rivers were clean, clear and pure.

We went with Bob while he surveyed, back and forth between these far distant parts of the Western United States we had all these places to play in and then back home at our hub of the universe, the Cayuse Ranch, we had the 4000 acres to roam. We were mostly camping out but always on horseback. Bob used to say with a wink and a grin, "When I'm not in Wyoming I'm only camping out."

We had to stay in sight of the camp when very young, then when we were older, Gennevieve, Bob and Uncle Frank would say: "Keep looking back for landmarks so you can find your way back".

The Yellowstone Park, Jackson Hole, and the Tetons were wilderness with very few highways or graveled roads; mostly dirt ruts that wound between the trees and rocks. The brown bears would catch a huge fish from the rivers or lakes, then take the fish upon the highway to eat it, stalling traffic for miles. The Park Rangers were helpless to move the bear to clear the highway. Then Bob done his thing - slow and easy Bob would walk up there behind the bear as he done his special sounds and shuffle as he pushed the bear off the highway - the bear still eating the fish. (Don't try it!)

When we were in Jackson Hole and Jenny Lake, etc., the brown bears were plentiful. A brown bear would often get into the cook-tent for food. Uncle Frank would look before going in the tent, then if a bear was there, he would take a dishpan or kettle and a spoon, from the campfire area, then go to the back of the tent to beat on the dishpan scaring the bear so it ran out of the tent and away

Once when Emmett and I were coming back across the timbered ridge behind where we were camped by Jenny Lake. we crossed trails with a Grizzly Bear. I was 20 feet or so following behind Emmett on a game trail, when I saw this Bear coming on another game trail that crossed our's. Emmett never saw the bear as he was a ways over on the other side of this trail. I stopped and stood very still while this bear went on by. The bears shoulders were higher than this 4 years old's head. Bob and Mama were upset (so was the whole camp) when they heard that this bear was so close to us and the camp. I didn't worry about it as I was used to having bears around. I just didn't know about grizzlies.

Bob talked about my going "where Angels fear to tread"

July 4th, we were lighting fire-crackers. I was cornered by three boulders then Emmett and another boy were beside me so I couldn't throw the firecracker down or anywhere - while I was thinking of dropping it, the firecracker went off in my hand tearing the flesh away . We could see the bones in the palm of my hand and my fingers. A nurse, who lived on a nearby ranch came by every day to put a fresh bandage on my hand. She used a mixture of flour, pure white lard, and fresh country cream for the dressing. They said it would keep the infection out and my hand would heal up nicely, it did.

There were two women who came, each day, one was the nurse, the other came with the fresh cream. One was Mrs. Grey, and one rode a grey horse, I don't remember if it was Mrs. Grey who rode the gray horse. Uncle Frank had the flour and the lard... in his cooktent with the cooking supplies. We were seldom injured, and never sick unless someone went to town and brought back the germs. Bob had Blue Vitriol, Epsom Salts and Iodine in his little tin box where he kept important papers and things.

We were camped along a creek below a huge glacier.

Uncle Frank went up on the glacier and saw a crevasse and heard it creaking and making an awful noise as if it would break off any day and we were camped below it. Frank warned the Chief of Party, Murphy, who said they would wait to move until they were done mapping there. The next day or so we moved. A day later some of the crew went back to get some stuff that they had left and found where we had been camped was 10 feet under water. A piece of the glacier had broke off and fell into the lake. We would of been swept away if still camped there. We were warned in time.

When we moved we usually had both cars, the Durant and the Whippet and pulled a homemade two wheeled cart that was made from an old pickup box. Bob bought the Durant from Bill and Ruby Wesley for $700. It had low mileage so we went to Iowa to see Aunt Liz, then a short time after that we went to California. This could of been the time in California when Emmett was very sick. The doctor said Emmett would not get better. We waited around for him to die, but decided couldn't wait any longer so took off for home with the sick boy. As we come down over the divide into Nevada, Emmett stood up and was okay, well again. Same thing happened when we were out in Washington when Dipper was a baby; the doctor said no hope that I was dying. They couldn't wait around any longer, had to get home to Cayuse Ranch, Coming down the mountains into Montana, I sat up and then stood up in the car, well, again. They thought it was the damp weather as it rained all the time we were there.

1937 we went to Lander, Moran, and Pinedale; Nejl was born there in Lander. When we went through The Wind River Cave the Indian guide showed us a burial place there in a side tunnel. Mama crawled in and took a piece of the blanket, also a piece of the saddle, things the Indian would need on his journey to heaven. The Guide begged Mama not to take anything as the Indians have a curse that anyone who disturbs their graves will die young. Saw Bi-planes with stunt fliers doing loop-de-loops. Saw women walking the wings of these two-winged planes.

Sometimes we, too, climbed the mountain peaks, our legs aching but Bob would say, "Come on, you can make it, the view from the top is worth it."

The mountainsides and meadows were full of wild flowers; Bob said, "that Solomon and all his glory was not arrayed like one of these". Sometimes Bob said, that Solomon asked for Wisdom and got all other riches besides."

Then to Sacramento, and San Luis Obisgo. Saw the Shallows return to San Juan Capristrano. Went to church in those old Spanish Missions founded by Fr. Jumperio Sierra. Rode the street cars in San Francisco, saw the Golden Gate Bridge when it was new. Saw the circus, too. Bob drove the car through the highway tunnel through one of giant redwood trees, in Sequois National Park.

Around the campfires in the evenings we looked at the

116

moon, stars and planets through Uncle Frank's Telescope; then went to the observatories to see the planets through the large lens. Tubby, Bob's dog, went with us all over the West, on all these trips. Tubby rode on the front fender of the car, wrapping his front feet around the headlight, hanging on while he watched the road ahead. We lost Tubby in Los Angeles, as he may have went 'wild' to join the coyotes. We waited for Tubby to return and looked for him but had to leave without him.

1937 and '38, were in Arizona and Death Valley; where Bob earned the name of 'Desert Rat' because he could stand the heat. Bob often returned to camp at night with his face sunburnt with his lips black and cracked open. Campfire stories of Scott's Follies and other lost gold mines. Saw the Indian dances at Pow Wow's; also saw their Sun Dance.

Bob and Gennevieve took us to see Mount Rushmore when 'The Faces' were being built. We saw the scaffolding hanging down over The Faces with people working on them. Also saw some blasting.

When Bob was in Texas, he had the keys to the King ranch. As he was the Ambassador of Good Will all over the Western States for the United States Geological Survey-- Topographic Branch. On all these trips, Bob was sent ahead to make arrangements for the Survey Party to be on their land, whether on the Indian Reservations or other private property.

While Bob was on these surveying trips, our Mama's brother, Cecil was with us some of the times, other times he would be running the Cayuse Ranch, Uncle Ferdie would run the three ranches some of these trips; one summer Charley Williams and his family put up the hay and took care of things in general.

Mom and Dad studied the history of the places and areas that our Dad would be surveying, then told and showed us children. So we were so blessed to have seen the places and the people, as we camped and learned, we were not just traveling through. --- Dipper

Frank and Fae Married

What did Frank do? Being Bob's baby brother, he married Gennevieve's baby sister, Fae. After that Bob called Frank, "His little brother-in-law"

Uncle Frank married Aunt Fae in 1938: At the Catholic Church in Newcastle, Wyoming. A big Wedding Dance was held for them at Oshoto, in the hayloft of Bill and Ruby Wesley's barn. Sure a big event, with all the neighbors there. Nadine Chittim Rankin told me that her brother, Charley Chittim, was one of the Band who played that night. --- Dipper

The Lost Wallet

In the White Silver Sands Desert. New Mexico I remember playing in the sand by the side of the road made of slabs of boards laid across the loose sand.

Bob lost his wallet there. We searched under boards, in the sand, behind and under the car seats. Everyone looked for days, the house was searched. This was the money we needed to get home on. Bob prayed to St. Anthony. Once again Bob looked between the front seat and the back rest. This time it was found!

We saw the Bats fly out of the Carlsbad Caverns. New Mexico. Spent a winter in Tucson, Arizona. Bob and Emmett had pneumonia. The doctor had them coming to his office every day for treatments of laying under the heat lamp for an hour or so. After a few times of this Bob decided the Arizona sunshine would work just as good and cost a lot less; so they took their blankets and layed out in the sun along side of our house and soon recovered.

Then back to Rock Springs and Green River, Wyoming. Some time in here we were in Utah, saw the Rainbow Natural Bridge, the red buttes in Monument Valley, and we floated in the salt water of the Great Salt Lake. We all had balled-faced tires when on these trips but Ray Bellows used folded up newspaper for `boots' in his tires; these `boots' showed through the tires. Bob said, "that anyone could drive a new car, but it took a real genius to drive an old car, to hold it together to get where one was going."

Traveling times were tough! If the car broke down, we had to stay there along side the road until they got it fixed. If had a flat tire, they patched it with a kit, used the hand-pump to pump the air back into the inter-tubes. But we never knew times were tough. Mama and Dad made the trips fun for us; so many things to see and do. The campfires stories and singing, Mama played her violin, Uncle Frank played his mouth-harp... Harmonica, and also his violin. Bob would sing the old cowboy songs. We had all the Western United States to play in, then when back on the Cayuse Ranch, we had 4000 acres to roam.

We had to stay in sight of camp when we were young, then when older Bob and Uncle Frank would say, "Keep looking back for landmarks, so you can find your way back to camp."

Gennevieve drilled us on the directions, on which way was North, South, East or West. For several years after Bob lost Chopo and Hoot he would watch the ridges and hilltops for them. Especially Banshee Mtn. and the hill southwest of the ranch buildings. Like he half-way expected them to come over it and stand on top at sunrise to survey the ranch below, just as Grand Dad `Rarey Fir' did when he came when they homesteaded there - just as Bob did when he walked out from Moorcroft the 30 miles when he came home from France after World War I. Just as Emmett and Nejl did later when they returned from the Korean War. When Emmett came home on leave, he borrowed a horse from Charley Williams at Moorcroft, delivered some horses out to Wind Creek for Charley; went to a dance along the D Road; then was on the hilltop at daylight. Rode 80 miles so wore the hair off his legs, as he hadn't ridden while in the Army. When Emmett was Discharged from the Army he drove his car home but stopped on the D Road, other side of the hill, to walk to the top at sunrise to look over. Nejl walked barefoot the 30 miles from Moorcroft during the night, he had trouble with people coming by wanting to give him a ride home, but he walked and was there at sun-up. Bob heard that Chopo and Hoot got as far as Casper and were kept in a stockyard there waiting for the owner to show up to claim them - but when we heard about them - .they were already gone. Bob said "Anyone would take Hoot as he was beautiful and anyone could ride him. But Chopo was hard to handle and not just anyone would be able to get along with him, so Bob was afraid he would go a different route and possibly go through the sale-ring to the killer market... but then maybe not." by Dipper

A Trail Home from Colorado

One fall when it was time to break camp and head for home, the survey Chief of Party left two others with Bob to trail the twenty head  of horses home. Had to trail through Brown's Hole. Still a wild country, an outlaws hideout, as it is in the three corner area and the outlaws could always run to a different state. They had to pack up all the belongings and move out. First one man made an excuse that he had to leave and since there was still two men to bring the horses, he would go on home. Wasn't long before the second man received the message that he was needed at home - a death in the family; so he had to get on home. - then he left, too. That left Bob alone to bring the horses. It was quite a chore to pack up all the camp and pack the horses each morning and then unpack

121

them at night. ---Dipper

Section Eight

The Fork in the Road – Saving the Spanish Mustang

The Fork in the Road

1940-1943. When a man came to tell Bob he couldn't continue with the United States Geological Survey--Topographic Branch; the people had to have a college degree to work there now. Required these men who had been doing the job of mapping for 30 years or more to go back to school to college to get a degree. Bob wanted to go and missed being on these trips, but they never called him again. Whatever happened to the thousands of years of apprentice-ships where young people worked to learn a trade?

1943: Then came the Fork in the road, Gennevieve had died. Bob's friends on Survey were going back to College so that they could continue to work for the United States Geological Survey- Topagraphic Branch. Bob took the road least traveled to stay home to keep his family together. Then began the search for the pure Spanish Horses.

Years before this Bob had searched for the horses for use on the Survey. For years I remember Bob talking to people "that the Spanish horse was being exterminated, that very few, if any, were left in the world." He kept saying that someone ought to do something to preserve these horses.

Other people might have asked Bob "Why didn't he do it?" But the turning point was when a surveyor friend and co-worker, Jim Clark of Bozeman, Montana came to visit and said, "that you , Bob, have the knowledge, experience , and the ranch-land to run the horses on, it looks like it is up to you to preserve the Spanish Horse." John Blackburn also urged Bob to save the true old time Spanish Horse.

When Ping and Pong where getting older, Blackburn said this: "Gather up the horses like Ping and Pong and preserve them from extinction." People kept saying to Bob, "Someone ought to start a preserve or a registry, do something to preserve these horses so a valuable part of our history wouldn't be lost".

When Bob decided to preserve the Spanish ponies, in the early 1940's, he said, "If you want a job done and want the job done right, do it yourself." So he did - saying "although others (registries) are doing and using all bloodlines, using inbreeding which they call `line-breeding', we have to bring these ponies back pure,"without a hair-turned"

Then had to prove it. Bob started his search --- if he could find any ponies left. It has been said, In every age there is a man (woman) to be the right man, the right time, the right place; with the help from God and alittle bit of luck he will be alive to do it." In this case, to save the original Spanish pony/horse from extinct-ion, **Bob Brislawn the Man!** Bob succeeded where many had tried and failed. Later on when Bob made The Spanish Mustang Registry, he made it a non-profit corporation so people wouldn't say he founded The Spanish Mustang Registry for profit. The Lord only knows the money and years spent in searching out the far places for the purest of the last of a breed. ---Dipper

The Search

"Seek and you shall find" (Matthew 7: 7-8) .... goes the Bible verse and Bob certainly seeked for the last remaining remnants of the Spanish Mustangs

Those were the times and places where Bob lived and surveyed. Bob said he saw Will James on a train they were both traveling on, and that he knew Charley Russell.

Bob Brislawn never had college degrees after his name from reading books. Never the less, Bob HAD read the books, had researched the material and also had the lifetime experience of working with the horses and history of the United States of America, so knew the horse and the people from the inside out. He knew them from being out there among them, in the dust, sweat and tears.

In the days when a man could do more than one job on the United States Geological Survey, Topographic Branch, Bob was at times, topographic engineer and surveyor. He drew the hills and creeks on the contour maps so well that, 30 or 40 years later, when the Government sent back into the country a new batch of surveyors, college graduates with degrees after their names, with sophisticated instruments, there were very few changes made on the maps.

The Chief of Party would state, "Take Bob, as he can do all phases of the surveying from engineer to rod-man, to packer and teamster and has a string of pack horses who could go where the mountain goats can't." Bob also acted as interpreter on the Indian Reservations. and acted as an Ambassador of Goodwill, wherever they went.

Later Bob was a guest speaker at universities and colleges all over the Western United States: he had many articles published and was written about in many and various magazines and books, from all over the world. However, none ever mentioned nor told of the seventeen years search and research, heartaches, willow-bark and pinto beans done by Bob and his children before they could form a registry.

Many years later, when people formed other registries on the Indian or Mustangs Horses they did not have all the hardships that the Robert E. Brislawn Sr. family had.

Other registries didn't have to go though all that: people just went and drew up the paperwork with a lawyer and said they had formed a registry. They never had to struggle.

When other people started registries of their own on the Spanish Horses/Mustangs, some were founded on endurance or the Barb or the Indian types, not purity. As far as I know, none of these people had to prove anything about their horses over a period of years before forming or founding a registry, like we did in 1957, when founding the Spanish Mustang Registry, Inc.

The Spanish Mustang Registry, Incorporated, was the first and only registry based on the purity of the remnants of the Spanish Horse. Other people are NOT concerning themselves over the purity of their horses, which explains WHY there are both Tobianos and Overos in their string. (Tobiano is a color phrase of the Shetland from Great Britain and the Overo is the Spanish Pinto.) In spite of that these people are saying they are perpetuating the Spanish Horses/mustangs.

People can see the Shetland bloodlines, conformation and coloration of the Tobiano and so say. "If the Tobianos are in these people's herds, they must be Spanish Horses, so good enough for me..."

Wrong. A Spanish horse never had the markings or coloring or conformation of a British, Scottish, or Shetland horse. Farmers, ranchers, and horsemen know that, but I don't know why the college students have been so misinformed. Bob wrote "'Lets Honor the Shetland', but lets not use him in our Spanish Mustangs, he's a different breed of horse." So, to maintain purity, the Spanish Mustang Registry registers only the Overo pintos.

In the writer's club I was told that "Writer's have `Poetic license'. You can write anything, it doesn't have to be the truth". (A license to lie?) But, I've kept to the truth.

It's the same way with the artists. They paint the Indians on horses of Quarter Horse and Shetland Pony conformation with the coloration of pintos, paints, pie-bald, Spanish Pintos, war bonnets and medicine hat markings of the Spanish Mustang. Once it was the exactness of what was there at the time. Once things had to be the truth. Artists like Charley Russell, O. C. Seltzer and Ferderic Remington painted the exactness of what they saw.

The movies and television show Indians and cowboys coming Yip, yip, yipping down the hills on large horses with the wrong conformation and coloring, not of the old-time Spanish Mustang.

Today, the Indians are painted in pictures by artists and shown in the movies and on television on Tobiano paint horses, but the Shetland came later after the Spanish horse was well distributed across the country. Let's honor the Shetland Tobiano color and markings; but he's a different breed of horse from the Spanish Medicine Hats and War Bonnets. The Spanish horses have different markings, from conformation, eyes, roan hairs,"tufts" of hair in the ears, to the markings on their feet. Perhaps it takes a learned eye to see that. In a movie in which Bob was an extra, the producers couldn't find a horse with the right color and conformation, so simply used a white horse and painted on the Medicine Hat markings as well as the Indian's medicine symbols. The movies even show horses that are supposed to be wild unbroken range horses but with saddle marks on them. Do they fool anyone?

Many things mentioned in the books are wrong; people are misinformed by the misinformed, and just pass it on. It's the same with teachers in our schools. Bob would ask the question,

"How can people teach what they haven't done?"

It seems that learning from the pages of a book isn't enough ... they get misinformed. People need to learn not only from the pages of a book, but also, from someone who has been out there, "their faces marred by dirt and sweat," as the great Teddy Roosevelt said.

The Williamses

Oshoto, Wyoming 1940's: Bob gathered up the remnants of the mares from the herd that Charley Williams, his brother Dick and Dick's wife, Leva, in 1925, trailed down from Wyola, Montana to Moorcroft,

Wyoming. These horses were from the Crow Indian Reservation. Charley Williams' son, Chuck, told me this April 29, 1995: "Leva was as good, or better, a hand then most men so rode with them. This was a scary trip, as Leva's first husband had threatened to kill them for what she had done; when she divorced him and married Dick. But the first husband never came, he left to go off some place else to live. and never bothered them."

The Williams camped by Spotted Horse, Wyoming for a few days on their trail down. Chuck said, that "Charley leased, or had a deal, to live on the Butte Ranch near The Little Missouri Buttes, so had a place to live before going back for his family. Dick and Leva didn't go back."

"Then Charley and his oldest son, worked together on the Butte Ranch." "Also a Bohemian worked with them. The Bohemian found a gold nugget when digging a post hole; they looked and looked for more gold but none was ever found." Of the horses that had been trailed down, all the mares had been sold and horse colts gelded and sold until the only two horses that Charley had left were Pigeon, a bay gelding and Kate, a dark sorrel mare. Pigeon was Kate's colt. Chuck said, "Charley's wife, Nina, owned Pigeon." "All the Williams' children rode Pigeon and learned to ride on him." "Charley used Pigeon as his saddlehorse and used him for roping and the all around ranch work.

"The Williams had Pigeon for many years as they still had him when they moved to Moorcroft, Wyoming," Chuck told me. Kate had another colt they called "Old Bill". Nellie, Charley's sister, might of had `Old Bill' before her and Vonley Johnson were married. They sold `Old Bill' to Charley Reynolds. `Old Bill' was smaller than Pigeon but Charley Reynolds rode him for many many years and done everything on him. Old Bill was a good horse except hard to get on, as he took off fast. Old Bill was about the same color as Pigeon but a darker Bay,

When the Williams lived on the Pollack Place they still had Kate, a sorrel mare. Mildred Sherwood was boarding with Williams the winter of 1942/1943 when she was teaching the Brislawn School when it was located over along the D Road. Everyday, Mildred rode Kate the 6 or 7 miles over there and back.

There were many different colors of horses in the herd that was trailed down, but one was of the Medicine Hat color. The Williams have always been friends and encouraged us all the way, in the preservation of the old time Spanish Horses. If Charley, Dick and Leva hadn't of trailed these horses down they wouldn't of been there either. Leaving Bob to gather up the few remaining remnants of the Williams's mares: Kate, Bob bought from Charley Williams, 3 miles away. Penny, Bob bought from Charley Reynolds, 8 miles away. Queenie, Bob bought from Bill Glover who lived over the hills across the New Haven County Road. about 7 or 8 miles away. Emmett rode her home, gave her a feed of oats and turned her out with the rest of our saddle horses. Next morning she was gone! Bob figured she would try to go back to Glovers so went up to- wards Uncle Frank's place thinking he would catch-up with her. Bob asked Uncle Frank if he saw anything of her....."Yes, he had but when he tried to catch her-- she threw up her heels and high-tailed it towards Glovers, jumping the fence and getting away." She made it all the way back to Glover's over at least 9 fences; two being the County Road lane fence where she would not have a running start, others being sheep-tight fences. Queenie didn't have a wire cut or mark on her. Emmett had to ride her home again. His legs weren't long enough to reach the stirrups to get on so he would grab the saddle strings and climb on. Bob, with the rest of us, drove the old Terraplane car along the road as close as he could to help Emmett at the gates.

Emmett beat us home both times, as he could go faster across country 'a horseback' then we could in the car. After that Queenie made her home at Cayuse Ranch, until she moved to Utah with Bob in 1961. Emmett and I used to jump the fences when riding Queenie but that didn't solve our problem with the gates as the horse the other was riding wouldn't jump fences!

That was Queenie; a blue roan Medicine Hat mare, SMRI #8. Topsye SMRI #34, was out of Arizona Spanish Mustang stock brought to Wyoming in 1908 by the 101 Ranch of Moorcroft. Bob bought Topsye from Hysham of the Flying E Ranch, Moorcroft, Wyo. We had some mares, but no stallions! Summer of 1943, Oshoto, Wyoming:

Bob and Emmett caught up their ponies, Tim and Tyee, to go in search of an old white Indian mare someone said was up along the Montana Border on Parks Land and Cattle Company ranch, now Rockypoint Grazing Association, near Rockypoint, Wyoming, 25 or 30 miles North of us. Emmett was eleven years old. Three times they went spending three days each time. They unrolled their bedrolls and camped for the nights wherever they happened to be in our northern climate it was awful cold. Our schoolteacher, Mildred Sherwood, stayed with us younger children that first time, after the death of our mother. We spent the next two times with Uncle Frank and Aunt Fae. Emmett rode Old 'Paint' once but Bob rode 'Tim' each time. The third time Dad and Emmett rode in searched for that old white Indian mare, it rainned all the time they were gone. They were thirty miles from home with a cold rain and darkness falling as they rode up to Pete Pitts place on Lightening Flats -- Bob wah-whooed but no one was home. (Bob had a distinct voice which would carry for miles when he yodeled 'Wah-who' like he did during the survey days when the horses were grazing away from camp. Dad would start out in the direction of the tracks following their sign and every so often he would Wah-who, when the horse heard him from off in the distance they would come running in for their oats.)

As Emmett and Bob were wet and cold they put their ponies in the barn which was part open shed that was built into the side of a cut-bank so that one wall was dirt. Lighting a lantern which hung from the rafters, they stood around in the barn waiting for Pete Pitts to return, finally deciding he must not be coming they went to the homestead shack, in the custom of the Old West, starting a fire in the cook-stove, the coffee was boiling when Pete came riding in - Emmett was uneasy about being there but Bob went to the door and hollared, "Put your horse away, supper is just about ready." When Bob explained what they were doing there and their search for that old white Indian mare. Pete told them where he had last seen her - .on a certain draw on Lightening Flats.

After spending the night there, they rode out to that draw -- only to find the mare lying down and dying. That search was in vain.

Bob and Emmett continued the 30 mile ride home arriving to find that one year old Shane was near death with pneumonia. No chance of getting to town tonight in the dark with muddy roads; wait until tomorrow morning to start out for a doctor. Early the next day Bob loaded all five of us children into the old Terraplane car with Shane bedded-down on the backseat and started to get help in Moorcroft, Wyoming 28-30 miles away. The D Road was nothing more than a trail bladed by bulldozer through the sagebrush so that the rainwater or snow laid in the low areas making travel worse. The road wound its way on contours of the hills, up and down and around. and was very muddy as there had been rain for several days. Part of the road was sandy soil so no trouble. We got stuck in the mud in most of the draws but by cutting sagebrush and putting it under the wheels we kept going until Miller Creek. The three or four miles across Miller Creek flat looked hopeless to cross. there was red gravel on the road on the otherside of that flat if we could only make it. The gumbo mud was rolling, sticking to the tires. Lost the tire-chains several times so while Bob chopped more sagebrush for under the wheels, Emmett, Nejl and I looked for the chains by dragging our feet in the muddy ruts to feel for the chains as very difficult to see them. Bob said, the mud would look different, that it might look like chain links, or just a little lumpier in one spot. In that road of muddy ruts, some ruts were filled with rainwater, it seemed hopeless but we did find the chains, everytime. Once Nejl found the chains in a puddle of muddy water, after everyone else had spent a lot of time looking for them and had given up. We would go to look in on Shane sleeping in the backseat all covered up with blankets - while 4 year old Colleen was playing in the front seat. We had come 2/3's of the way, about 20 miles, through a lot of bad spots on draws and steep hills but Miller Creek flat looked hopeless as we stood in the rain looking out across that long stretch of flat and the muddy road, if we could only make it across, the road was graveled from there with red-tinder gravel from pits near Gillette.

It took several hours to go that 3 or 4 miles to the gravel where we had clear going to Highway 14-16. Looking back across that flat it looked like it was paved with sagebrush Bob had cut. It sure felt good to be on solid gravel road when we got on it and even better to be on the highway. Then on to Moorcroft. We went by Charley and Nina Williams' just outside of Moorcroft.....Howard Arnold (Nina's brother) and Mildred Sherwood were married by this time and just returned from their Honeymoon, so were there. The sun started to shine and Shane's fever broke. Shane had survived!

That ordeal was the beginning of the agonizing decision to "Farm out" Shane - to get someone else to take care of Shane for a few years. Mildred Sherwood's mother took Shane for awhile, then the Knneppels', while they worked at the Bentonite Plant near Upton, Wyoming. On Sundays we attended Mass at St. Anthony's and visited Shane. done this for a year or two. It was a fifty mile trip one way. When the Knneppels moved to Ghadron, Nebraska, Shane came home to us. ---Dipper

Holbrooks

Fall of 1945 Montie and Sadie Holbrook and family came through the country trailing and trading horses on their way back to Maybelle and Craig, Colorado area. The Holbrooks camped overnight on Bob Brislawn's in the pasture of the big stockwater reservoir along the `D' Road, for food and water for their horse herd. Bob Holbrook said "that he would always remember when they were camped in our reservoir pasture along the road. That the next morning Bob Brislawn was standing there talking to his Dad, Monty, when they were dealing for Buckshot and Ute. "Bob Brislawn bought Buckshot, a two year old grullo stallion and Ute, born in 1943, a stocking legged blazed faced sorrel colt, for $25.00 a piece. Further north the Holbrooks had been getting $15.00 per head for the colts. Emmett would of been 10 years old at that time. At this time Ferdie was living near Casper, Wyoming and working in the Casper Post Office. So Ferdie most of gotten Ute from Bob later on. That was Buckshot, S.M.R.I. #1; and Ute, S.M.R.I. #2 and the two foundation sires of the Spanish Mustang Registry

Incorporated came from the Holbrook herd. Bob Holbrook, Monty's and Sadie's son, told me that he remembered when they were packed up and heading out that morning, he was riding a little Bay mare who bucked with him down over the bank of the dam and went into the Reservoir with him. He was riding an old Army McClellan Saddle, with a coat tied across in front of him so he could ride the bucking horses. ---Dipper

Gathering Up the Remnants. The Search Continues

About 1946 or 1947, I don't remember the year, when we were looking for the rare Medincine Hat horses, Bob was told by a man he met in a bar over there, that there were four Medicine Hats, that one mare had the sacred Eagle Feather marking in the flank. on a reserve for the Buffalo and other wild animals in the Custer State Park,South Dakota - but when Bob went to check into that bunch of horses they had all been shot two weeks before. There were 10 or 12 horses left laying to rot in a wide grassy canyon. The Medicine Hats ranged in age like the mare and her colts, down to the new foal. Others were sorrels, bays and grullos. Several men were with us, to show us this place.

One summer we went to Ekalaka, Montana (pop 663) to see Talkington's horses. They were mixed bloodlines - good horses but not what we were looking for. If you have never been on that road between Oshoto and Ekalaka you are really missing out -.it is all dirt road 135 miles long - except for one mile. 75 miles between Alzada and Ekalaka Montana. When we arrived we asked directions out to Talkington's and then we got a loaf of bread some Bolgna and cheese, drove out of town aways and found a place to camp. Colleen and I got to sleep in the car but Bob and the boys just unrolled their bedrolls on the ground along side of the car - really traveling in style! That is the way we traveled.

Done the same way everywhere we went searching for these horses. or before when on the survey. 35/40 miles per hour was top speed on those roads in those days. ---Dipper

Section Nine

Some hardships

The Blizzard

January 1, 1949: A beautifull winter day. Uncle Frank took us in his jeep back to Moorcroft to catch the Trailways Bus to Saint Joseph's Orphanage, Torrington, Wyoming where Nejl, Colleen, Shane and I were boarding while going to the Public School there. We had been home for the Christmas vacation. The worst storm in our history hit us that evening. Bob, Emmett, Uncle Frank, Aunt Fae, Dennis, Karen and Mack got as far as Garman's on the Cabin Creek Road, (the D Road was blocked with snow so they had to go around by Carlile.) Left Aunt Fae and the children there as Uncle Frank thought he could make it on home, but only made it to Oshoto.

Uncle Rrank, Emmett and Bob spent the next 3 or 4 days there at Ruby Wesley's before the storm was over and they walked on home. They were snowed in for 28 days...before help came. The Trailways Bus got as far as Torrington, Wyoming by four a.m.; so still dark and storming. The streets were lighted by the streetlights so we could see our way across the 1/4 mile to the orphanage. The snow was swirling around our feet into drifts as we walked over to the Orphanage. All four of us held hands so we would not be separated. We went on in to the Reception Room and waited until morning. Father Stoll was scolding me for not getting him to come after us. I can't understand why, I was used to finding my way across the prairie with only the sagebrush to follow. Here I could see the huge lurking hulk of the four-story Orphanage building. A book could be written on this blizzard and all the Heroics of hero's and heroines' but will tell that tale another day. ---Dipper

Entries From Bob's Black Book

May 13, 1949: Winter broke right after February 20th and the nicest spring I ever seen. No killing storms. Grass short due to lack of moisture. Last winter storm Febr. 20. 1949. Still a few snow drifts on West sides of creeks. Hope they are still there for the Kids to see when they come home May 28th. ---Bob

Note: Uncle Frank lost his cow herd this winter. That spring or summer he bought the Clearmont Motel, in Clearmont, Wyoming and moved there with Aunt Fae, Dennis, Karen and Mack. ---Dipper

Nejl's Riding to School

January 16, 1951: Dry and dusty. No snowbanks in draws, just alittle on North slopes but none looking North. 40 degrees above most days. Good grass but a little moisture would do good. Emmett braking horses and Nejl riding to the Terry School 6 miles. Two Cayuses, Cricket and Nora, time 30 minutes. Has rode 1000 miles to date and hopes he is getting 10 cents per mile. No Isolation money as yet. ---Bob

Note: Rural Little Missouri School. Vivian Stainbrook was the teacher there, 1948/49 and 1950/51. ---Dipper

Colleen and Shane Rode to School Too

The school house was moved back along the D Road to be half way between Harold and Doroty Burches' and Bob's. About two miles for each family to come. Dennis, Mack and Karen Brislawn also went to this school, but the school wasn't half way for them. Frank drove his little army-surplus jeep to take his children the four miles to school. Across the road from the school, Bob built a small shed to put their horses in so the horses wouldn't have to be tyed to the fence standing outside during the cold blizzards of winter. Colleen and Shane rode to school, during these three years. They were young children so most of the time Bob took them over leading the horse they rode. Both on the one horse. Then went back about 4 o'clock to bring them home. One of the horses, they rode, was Queenie. (SMRI #8.) Brislawn/Burch School 1952/1953:

Arthur Dickson, of Dayton, Wyoming. taught the first year the schoolhouse was at this location. He was legally blind. Arthur came to Wyoming in a covered wagon and wrote a book about that. Arthur had a portable Organ and taught the students music along with the usual subjects. He had taught school many years of his life and took this portable School Organ to different schools teaching music. He later gave this little Organ to my sister, Colleen. This `Portable Organ' is on display at the Bob Brislawn Memorial Section of the Crook County Museum, Sundance, Wyoming. Brislawn/Burch School 1953/1954:

Leona Harper, Newcastle, Wyoming taught school this year.

Although there was a room built on to the back of the one room country schoolhouse part of the time she didn't stay there as she drove back and forth that 90 miles to teach. One morning Harold Burch was moving some cattle along the D road, when Leona came over the hill too fast to stop and came upon the cattle, she scattered cattle and calves and went into the ditch.. When Harold rode up to the car Leona said, "Why didn't you tell me yesterday that you were going to move cattle today?"

Bob said, "Did it take her that long to stop?" No one was hurt. Brislawn/Burch School 1954/1955: Jeannie Shepherd of Oshoto, Wyoming taught that year. Jeannie rode a horse over to school part of the time; drove over at other times. ---Dipper

Yellow Fox 1952

Oshoto, Wyoming 1952: We loaded up the old Terraplane car and headed out towards Montana....went through the reservations there and came upon some ponies. Some were okay - through just a few left as the Indians had either sold them or were eating them, also so many of mixed blood. We came to an encampment of Indians at Lame Deer, Montana. There were some horses in the corral. One was a beautiful buckskin colt that the kids had riding around there. He was only a colt at the time he was ridden bareback by the small children. There were washtubs full of green wild-plums and horse meat over by the houses. Everyone was there for a Pyote celebration. They invited us to partake but we declined. I had the Rheumatic Fever, was all crippled up so couldn't walk. Bob carried me from the car to the corral and to the house where all the food was. Lots of Indians came to the car where I was, to talk awhile. We bought the colt and went home.

Uncle Cecil had to build a stockrack for his green 1937 Chevy pickup before Emmett and him went to Lame Deer to haul the colt home. Emmett said, they went by Ridge and cut off to Biddle, all wagon roads and sand blowouts. They had to stop and overhaul or work on the pickup before going on. Emmett wondered if they were going to get through. The Brand Inspection report just had on it, "Change of range to Wyoming." That was Yellow Fox, a buckskin stallion - SMRI #3.

Bob wrote in his Blackbook/journal: We brought Yellow Fox from a long haired Indian named Yellow Fox (Cheyenne Indian). Sire: small Buckskin stallion and mother: mare about the size of Queenie, maybe not as high withers. A light blue and red Pinto, same being at Lame Deer, Montana. ---Bob

Bob wrote to John Woodenlegs, Lame Deer, Montana. Wagon Boss for the Association on the Reservation. wanting to buy the mother of Yellow Fox. Postcard dated November 21, 1952, Dear Mr. Brislawn, I have received your letter, was surprised to hear from you and hoping you get well soon. I have sold the white filly. Yours Trully John Woodenlegs ---Dipper

The Oshoto Country

In the year of our Lord, 1953: We have a high standard of living and are very modern here-- to wit: The farmers have a floodlight to see their way to the back-house after dark. The passing of the horse was written 10 years ago by George Knotson and the Passing of the

Backhouse 60 years or more ago by James Whitmore Riley. Yet the Backhouse is still going strong more ways than one. ---Bob

Note: Bob was one of the first ranchers to sign up for the Rural Electric Association to build their powerline into our place but for some reason they didn't, and returned Bob's check for the cost of having the powerline built, into our place. There wasn't a telephone at our place, yet. Others had partyline phones. ---Dipper

March 23, 1953: Emmett made Casper OK. off to Army. Terrible wind and cold and dusty today. Hope we get April rains. ---Bob

Emmett was with Cash Minnick's mail stage to Upton from Sundance. The mail stage broke down couple of miles from Upton on that flat just north of the timber and town of Upton. Emmett just made the Bus for the Army Camp. but he made it. ---Emmett

Note: No money for gas, so people caught a ride with others going their way, usually with the mailman. That was why Emmett was with Cash Minnick on the way to catch a bus, out of Upton, for the Army. Emmett was in the Quarter Master Unit when they stilled used mules. ---Dipper

November 18, 1953: Amos, our dog, killed by car on D Road near gate. Automobile worst enemy of man, ruin more people, morally, physically, and financally then any invention since the Birth of Christ. ---Bob Note: We traded some goats to some people, who lived over by the Little Missouri Buttes, for that puppy. A cross between their Border Collie bitch and a wild coyote. People said he wouldn't be any good. that the wild coyote part would come out to dominate his instincts. But

142

it didn't - when we started using him to help me catch a chicken for our dinner, he would catch the chicken or turkey I pointed out and never bruised them. He never got to doing this on his own - just when we asked it of him. Amos never wanted his picture taken, he would always slink away to hide behind the house. When Amos was bitten by a rattlesnake, he went to lay in the blue mud at Jack's waterhole for 3 or 4 days, before coming home. ---Dipper February 13, 1954: Emmett, Dipper and Uncle Ferdie to leave by Bus for Spokane, tomorrow. Emmett to be in Camp Lewis, Washington on Febr. 19th. Warm like spring, 70 degrees. ---Bob

March 5, 1954: Emmett off to Japan or parts East. Dipper in San Diego. Raining tonight. (Emmett was on his way to Korea) ---Bob

March 10, 1954: Aunt Tat died at her home in San Diego. California. after a long illness of a Tumor on the Brain. Note: This trip to Spokane, Washington; Pendleton, Oregon; and San Diego, California was my belated High School Graduation present from Bob. I had recovered from the Rheumatic Fever, by then. Bob came out to his sister, Tat's, funeral then we caught a bus for home. ---Dipper

Section Ten

There Were Other People Interested

There Were Other People Interested – Founding the Spanish Mustang Registry

Among these struggles we were doing the research on the Spanish Horses. Burning the Midnight oil by kerosene lamplight. Besides my doing the cooking on the wood and coal stove, carrying water in and out, washing dishes, washing clothes on the washboard, breaking (training) horses, the pitching hay onto hay- racks and hauling in and driving the teams of horses, Bob was always asking me to run the horses into the corral as someone might of just drove in from Illinois, Montana or Texas - from somewhere - to take a `look see' at these rare horses and what they could do. It seemed we were feeding the multitudes: with 6 or 7 extra people there for breakfast; 32 people for noon meal; then 36 different people at supper - .different people for each meal. I have it in my diary. That was a little unusual, but I could hardly get the bedding washed and put back on the beds in the Teacherage between overnight guests. The dust of one vehicle leaving wouldn't be settled before another would come driving in. (Bob had bought the Teacherage by this time.)

Remembering when things and times on the Cayuse Ranch, got

144

busy with people, people, people and horses, horses, horses, Bob would wink at me while saying "they will have to sleep sometime". then we can get on with the research." and the business with the horses, of founding the Spanish Mustang Registry to preserve and save the remnants of the Spanish horses, the horse who built America. Charley Russell, the famous Cowboy Artist, said it best, "It was the horse who brought us out of the Caves!" (The Charles M. Russell Book, by Harold McCracken.) Bob was getting 400 to 450 letters of inquiry per month about the horses, from all points of the compass, so every spare minute was used in answering these letters. nearly always working until midnight. Sometimes Bob would quote: "The heights by great men reached and kept, were not attained by sudden flight, But they, while their companions slept, we're toiling upward in the night." ---Longfellow

We were doing lots of research, by reading the old books on the early-days history of North and South America and the drawings, paintings and photographs of the people and of their horses. I studied the Spanish and Latin languages in high school so I could read the Old Ships Logs and journals of Columbus, DeSota, Cortez and others, when the horses were brought over, so we would know what they said, not what someone else said they said. We had a book on the Spanish horses in South America, too. ---Dipper

Ilo Belsky

We corresponded with a lot of people who were interested in saving the Spanish Horse. One of those was Ilo Belsky of Eli, Nebraska. Bob and Ilo wrote back and forth for years about the different types and what points were needed to be a Spanish Horse, they agreed on most everything. Ilo was more interested in the cowpony type and later wanted to call the registry the Cow-pony Registry. Bob went down there and bought one of Ilo's mares. Later Ilo had an annual meeting of the Spanish Mustang Registry, and was a member. Ilo Belsky has passed on but Tom Gaskins and Earl Wessel are gathering up Ilo's research work and many letters from Bob, while continuing the bloodlines of the Ilo Belsky horses. February 18, 1955 and a pretty tough Blizzard. 5 degrees below zero. Dipper and Shane rode Nora and Queenie to Jack's. Uncle Cecil out like summer. But he has hair on his chest and can face into the wind like a Buffalo. ---Bob

Note: Shane and I rode down to gather the cattle to help Uncle Cecil feed the hay to the cows. ---Dipper

July 14, 1955: Dipper and Nejl off to Toledo, Ohio with 7 Spanish ponies plus one half breed Morgan, same has feathers on her legs. All's well if a Rancher has his kids, a team of horses and a couple of saddle horses he hasn't a worry or a care. especially if he should have a sympathetic wife on the squaw type that never say. "Where in Hades have you been", if gone a little long. J. Frank Dobie is right we should have married with the Indians instead of certain Europeans. Less Communism. The Indian loved freedom and had the gray matter or sense in the head. The Indian had something to live for besides sex. Too many today are down to just wine, sex and cars. Anyway, let us hope that they find the end of the rainbow--? They won't. The New World bred men that were neither lured or restrained by women. Men subduing wilderness and savage tribes. Butchering Buffalo, digging gold, pumping gold out of the earth. If men without women, then of men into whose imaginings women had hardly entered. these men are

146

gone like the mustang. Men looking for matchless mustangs, mines, fur and adventure. A wealth that is substantive and has nothing to do with loveliness or beauty. J. Frank Dobie said something to this effect. ---Bob

August 3, 1955: Moorcroft, Wyoming: Nora's time in Barrel race 23 seconds plus. Beat the McInerney quartermare, both Proctor hors- es, the Ripleys and Moore horses. The 2nd day Nora very lame in shoulder -- time 27 seconds. The brush races on the river 1953 - 54: Cricket's time 20-21 seconds for 2/10th mile and her best time for the Quarter mile 26 and 27 seconds. The Quarterhorses that were down on the river time for the Quarter mile -- 30 seconds.---Bob Note: When I was Rodeo Queen of Moorcroft Rodeo those two years it wasn't a beauty contest but I had to compete and wim. I rode Nora in those barrel races. The barrels were spaced further apart than they are now. Some horses are now running the barrels in 17 seconds, the horses might be faster now but the big differ- ence is the shorter distance between the barrels. In the cow cutting/penning event I rode Minnie Pearl, a horse I had trained myself. We cut out a steer from the herd and put it in the corral at the other end of arena. Shane rode Cricket in the brush race - he won, even though he wasn't watching at the start so Cricket took one turn around a telephone pole before heading out for the finish line. ---Dipper

December 27, 1955: Cecil and Colleen home from Dayton for Christ-mas. --- Bob

Note: January 1, 1956 when Uncle Cecil and my sister, Colleen returned to Dayton, Wyoming I went with them, to attend Heiman's Business College in Sheridan, Wyoming. Cecil was taking care of

Arthur Dickson, a blind teacher and pioneer to Wyoming, who had taught our school the year before. Colleen was attending Junior High School. I was able to complete the 3 year course during that one year, while I was working as a secretary for the Big Horn Realty, a real estate and insurance agency. More midnight oil--more studying. ---Dipper

Oshoto, Wyoming, June 1956: Lawrence P. Richards, Ph.D, Professor of Zoology, then of Pocatello, Idaho, first came to the Cayuse Ranch. Larry first contacted Bob as he was writing his doctoral thesis on the Spanish Horse/mustang and needed more information. Bob needed him as we couldn't go to a Lawyer to have the legal papers drawn up to form an incorporated registry for the Spanish Horse. After all the research and knowledge of the horses, Bob needed a person with a few college degrees after his name. Larry and Bob had been corresponding for sometime before he came. Later Larry wrote about when he and his wife, Chris, first arrived at Cayuse Ranch, that "the Great Spirit spoke during that tremendous thunder storm, with blue-black sky, with lightning striking, and the thunder crashing. We all went out to meet them at their car by the yard gate. Bob said, "You brought the rain, that the prairie needed it, and that the antelope, the mustangs, and cattle needed it. The buffalo were gone." ---Dipper

Oshoto, Wyoming 1956: Emmett came home from the army and leased the Cayuse Ranch so Bob could be free to go in search for the purest of the last Spanish Horses. ---Dipper

Oshoto, Wyoming 1956: May or June or there abouts: Nejl graduated from High school. Nejl went to the army, a month or so after Emmett came home from the army. Nejl was in the army 4 years, 1956 to 1960. He was stationed stateside during the Korean War. The High

148

School ROTC he had didn't count for the Louie. He was put in a bunch that had been in one week. His ROTC helped then. Those 3 months in Basic Training seemed as long as 3 years. ---Nejl, as told to Dipper December 3, 1993

Note: After Shane graduated from high school, he spent two years working in a Denver hospital. During the Korean War (or Peace Action, as it was called) there was a military `Draft', where every mother's son had to go unless they had a good reason for being needed at home. Bob had his sons, go out to work, like big corporations and business men do, especially with their eldest sons who would take over the leadership of the business so when they came back from working as a common laborer then could work their way up to run and understand their workers, if they themselves had worked their way through the ranks. ---Dipper

Tijeras, New Mexico, August 14, 1956: Living in Tom Gonzales 2 room house in Tijeras, N. Mexico. Have 5 horses here .---Bob

Gilbert and Bertha Jones

It was here in Tijeras that we met Gilbert and Bertha Jones, and their family. Gilbert had a line of Spanish Horses he had kept in his family. Here he had Dunny Boy, a 925 pound 14.1 hands yellow dun stallion. Foaled on LLano--Estacado 1932. Also had a few mares running on 10,000 acres of open-range.

A few years ago Gilbert told me that he had this line of horses but never once thought of making a registry to preserve the Spanish

Horse. Gilbert is a long time good friend of mine and the Brislawn family. He was a life-time member of the Spanish Mustang Registry, Incorporated.

Later on, at Finley, Oklahoma, he made the Southwest Spanish Mustang Association, Incorporated based on endurance and for endurance riding, not purity. He has some horses that will really go the distance. Gilbert and Bob searched for the remaining remnants in this area. There too, the Indians were clearing their ranges.

Bob had Homer Audrey, Gene Audrey's Uncle, watch the sale rings for the Spanish Horses, if he saw any that looked Spanish Bob would go check out the area those horses came from. January 1957: I came down to Tijeras. Colleen and Shane were riding the school bus into Albuquerque for school each day. Bob and I doing the researching, studying, writing letters in answer to the many inquiries, during the week then on week-ends we would drive through the Indian Reservations and all the remote places that a few old time mustangs might be hid away in and not be of mixed bloodlines.

When I first saw Cedro, she was pulling a walking plow for our next door neighbor, Louis Gonzales, who was plowing a field to plant corn. Hitched along with this cedar colored mare was a blue grey mare, Louis called Blue. Both Cedro and Blue were 13 1/2 - 14 hands, weighing 900 pounds or less. People in Wyoming would never use them to pull a plow as they would want a larger draft-type horse to do that. Cedro was used as a `woodhauler'. Men, women and children living in Tijeras and other settlements near the Sandia Mountains gathered up mesquite and cedar to be sold for firewood. They packed large piles of wood on these pon- ies, then walked to lead the pony the 15-20 miles to the town of Albuquerque to sell the firewood then return home the same day. That was Cedro, a redish ceder colored mare - SMRI #28.

Bob, Colleen, Shane and I drove all over New Mexico following leads, but to the same ending, no pure blooded horses when we got there - .all mixed bloodlines and we could see it at a glance! One day while waiting in a small village for the man that could tell us about the wild horse herd. We were sitting in the car in the shade of some trees - all the town kids came to visit and ask what we wanted. "Oh, Yes - everyone had a pony for us to see". Bob was kept busy with his `measuring stick - to satisfy them that their pony was not what we were looking for because it didn't measure up. It was hard for them to understand that since we were looking for Indian ponies that their pony wasn't an Indian Pony just because an Indian happened to own it!

Here too, Bob was called `Get the Stick' by the Indians. They told us to talk to Harvey Coleman, boss or foreman of the horses and cows on this reservation. He was a hard man to catch up with as he was usually out with the wagons on round ups. One time we tried to drive up into the Jemiz Mountains of New Mexico only to be stopped when the roads were closed from heavy rains....roads all washed out up in the mountain area....we had stopped at a small village to check the car's gas and oil be- fore heading on out to the mountains, there we were told that the roads were closed, no one able to get through, that a school bus of Catholic Nuns were stranded up in there, that no one was able to get through to find them to help them. We were still at this gas station when that school bus load of Catholic Nuns came in. They didn't recommend traveling that road at that time......so we never, but who knowns; did we miss a good horse because of that rain? No, I would rather think that God put a road block there so we would turn around and go back as on the way back home we stop- ped at the Santo Domingo Indian Pueblo..... The highway passed near the Santo Domingo Pueblo where I had visited before but Bob, Colleen and Shane had not. I said to Bob,

"I want you to see this Pueblo Trading Post". "We ought to stop there now as a long way back". Bob said, he had seen Indian trad- ing posts when they were really trading posts, not the tourist traps that so many are now." Maybe he was just tired from the long trip/drive we had had already that day. Since I was driving we went in.......pulled up in front of the trading post. Bob went in first, ahead of us. To our surprise the man at the counter was Harvey Coleman, the man we had been trying to locate for months! Harvey Coleman said, "Yes, they had a stud colt of those markings on their reservation", when Bob asked him about a Medi- cine Hat. If we weren't in a big hurry he could get him for us in the next year or so when the wagons went out on the round ups.

That was San Domingo, a Medicine Hat Stallion.. S.M.R.I. #4.

The Empty Graves

Tijeras, New Mexico, March or April 1957: We rented an adobe house from Tom and Louie Gonzalas, they were in their 70's. Louie told us he was raised in the same area that Billy the Kid was; that Billy the Kid was framed and credited for a lot of killings he didn't do in that Lincoln County Cattle War. That William Bonney was really a good kid and was not killed by his friend, Pat Garrett, who was the sheriff who supposedly killed the Kid. Louie said that those things where told, by Billy the Kids friends so the people would think that Billy was dead; then they would not be looking for him and Billy could leave the country to start a new life - the local Lincoln County people considered Billy the Kid a hero. Louie said that when he was young that he and a few of his friends, dug up the grave of Billy the Kid - the coffin was heavy when they pulled it from the ground, but when they lifted the lid the coffin was full of old harness and other pieces of junk! The same with Jesse James - Jesse lived on and even attended his own funeral as he looked in from the back of the room where his funeral services were being held - before riding on. Bob heard this from people who were there and knew - what was done. Also from Jesse James' grandson, Jesse James the III. ---Dipper

Oshoto, Wyoming, May 1957. Emmett didn't want to manage the Cayuse Ranch anymore so Bob, Colleen, Shane and I moved back from Tijeras, New Mexico. Emmett wanted to go ride with the wagons on the big ranches. So he did go later that summer. ---Dipper

The Spanish Mustang Registry Founded June 1957:

There was a heavy rain storm all of this week when a few brave men gathered at the Cayuse Ranch to put the final touch to the first rules and regulations for the registry for the preservation of these horse.

Bob and I had done all the correspondence with these people and others and had it written down. They only had to agree on them. - for the pure descendants of the horses raised 400 years ago especially for the conquering and conquest of the New World. This was when they put into effect all their past research and their plans for the future. The brave people who were there: Robert E. Brislawn (Bob), Lawrence P. and Chris Rishards, Ph.D's, Emmett, Colleen, Shane and myself. Nejl would of been there, but was in the Army so couldn't get away. Bob Racicot just happened to be there as he had stopped by to see the horses on his way back home to Montana after being discharged from the

Army. He was a special friend of the horses for many years after-wards.

Oshoto, Wyoming, June 14, 1957: The organizational meeting of the Spanish Mustang Registry, Incorporated. The 56 mile drive in the rain to the law offices of Attorney's-at-Law, Scotty Gladstone and Richard (Dick) Macy, Sundance, Crook County, Wyoming. All there was to do was to sign the legal papers and the by-laws for the Spanish Mustang Registry and it was then Incorporated. Bob and I had went in before this with the information from our years of research to Richard (Dick) Macy, Attorney-at-Law, who put it all into required legal form. and who had the papers ready to sign by Robert E. Brislawn, President; Emmett Brislawn, Vice- President, and Lawrence P. Richards Ph.D,, Secretary/Treasurer.

We had to prove what we said and done. We couldn't, and didn't, go to the lawyer to have the lawyer write up the Articles and the By-laws of Incorporation for the registration of the pure Spanish Horses, and then say, "There we done it". There has been other Mustang Registries formed since then but Bob's Spanish Mustang Registry, Incorporated, was the first registry for the Spanish Mustangs and the only one founded on the remnants of purity. They set out to preserve a breed of horses, not to create one. After 17 years of searching enough horses were found to make the registry. with 17 horses - as had been done for the South American Criollo Horses of Spanish origin in Chile in 1893; in Argentina in 1923; and Brazil in 1932 has been done for the horses in North America on June 14, 1957.

Only those three names on the Incorporation papers; as eldest son, Emmett was in as a founding father. Then in 1969, Bob gave the glory to his eldest brother, Ferdie, as founding father in the Spanish Mustang Registry's annual meeting held at Hamilton, Montana. In the tradition that the eldest son inherits the throne and they deserved every

154

bit of the glory. But the rest of us, Nejl, Colleen, Shane and myself, didn't get our suntan by sitting in the sun, but were out there riding the miles, driving the distance, digging through rotten carcasses of dead horses to prove the purity of the Spanish Mustangs. Yet, they have not received the recognition they deserve - as the privates in the ranks doing the fighting and working - as members. Nejl, in 1956, was in the army stationed at Fort Bliss, Texas; Visited Bob, Colleen and Shane in Tijeras, New Mexico that fall. At the time of the Organization meeting of the Spanish Mustang Registry June 14, 1957, Nejl was stationed at Niagara Falls, New York. Nejl was kept up to date on the goings on and had his say in all of what we were figuring on. When and how we decided on everything and what the horses should be. The name was a big discussion: Bob wrote Nejl a letter with this list of names. Cow Pony Registry; Cow Horse Registry; Spanish Pony Registry; Indian Pony Registry; Mustang Registry; Spanish Barb Registry; Barb Registry.

Nejl said he looked it all over and to make it all inclusive to cover everything sent us a letter, about a week before the meeting, suggesting the name Spanish Mustang Registry. Nejl thought that we would all be included in the corporation as founders but were not. Members were not mentioned. ---Dipper

The Foundation Stock

The three stallions:

Buckshot S.M.R.. #1 foaled 1943; a Grullo Stallion, blaze face, dark points. (Grullo is the color of the bird called the Sand Hill Crane, or the color of a mouse.) Sire: Monty (Buck) and Dam: Bally, S.M.R..

#35 from Monty and Sadie Holbrook horses. Owner: R. E. Brislawn, Oshoto, Wyoming.

Ute S.M.R.. #2 foaled 1945; Sorrel Stallion, bald face, white leg markings, Sire: Monty (Buck) and Bally, S.M.R.I. #35 of the Holbrook stock. Owner: F. L. Brislawn, Gusher, Utah.

Yellow Fox S.M.R.I #3 foaled 1952; Buckskin Stallion, black points, no dorsal stripe, Sire: Cheyenne Indian Buckskin. Dam: Cheyenne Indian Pinto. from the Cheyenne Indian Reservation, Lame Deer, Montana. Owner: R. E. Brislawn, Oshoto, Wyoming.

Of the seven mares only five were ever given a number, but pure, never the less: Queenie S.M.R.I. #8 foaled 1933. Blue roan Medicine Hat Mare: Sire Eagle, a buckskin and Dam: Sally, white. Charley and Dick Williams stock. Owner R. E. Brislawn, although Colleen Brislawn, claimed her.

Old Kate, a sorrel mare, mane and tail all same, no white markings and Penny, a bay mare with black points, foaled 1930's were from the Williams' stock, too, but never given a registration number. They should of been. Later their bones proved 100% correct. Their colts were registered.

Topsye S.M.R.. #34 foaled 1932 a Brown mare from the 101 Ranch, Moorcroft, Wyoming; Arizona Spanish Mustang. Owner: R. E. Brislawn, Oshoto, Wyoming.

Teton S.M.R.. #24 foaled 1942, a Purple Roan Mare, bald face, four stockings, black mane and tail, from the Shoshoni Indian Reservation, Wyoming. Owner: R. R. Brislawn, Oshoto, Wyoming.

Tim McCoy S.M.R. #30 foaled 1949, Bay Mare, crooked blaze, from the Red Desert of Wyoming. Owner: R. E. Brislawn, Oshoto, Wyoming.

Mexi Cali Rose S.M.R. #29 foaled 1951, a Buckskin Mare,

dorsal stripe, zebra markings, black points. From Old Mexico. Owner: Emmett Brislawn, Oshoto, Wyoming.

That was the core of the foundation stock the others were their colts -- their off-spring.

Mora, SMR #38, Grand Dam was Topsye SMRI #34.

Amarilla SMR #36, Grand Dam was Queenie SMRI #8.

Shortly afterwards Gilbert Jones registered his two: No 39 was S.M.R.'s `Miss Albuquerque', foaled 1946, an Orange Dun Mare, black mane and tail, dorsal stripe, Sire: Dunny Boy a buckskin, foaled 1932, and Dam: Buckskin Girl. Tijeras Lightening S.M.R. #40, foaled 1952. a Sorrel Mare, small star, dorsal stripe, Sire: Wild Mexican Stallion Dam: Gotch-eared Mare.

Terry Whitmore, Tijeras, New Mexico registered his mare Chip S.M.R. #16 foaled 1954. A Black Overo Mare, with roaning. Sire: Wild sorrel from Tijeras Mountain country. Dam: Black Spanish mare

The fourth stallion, San Domingo S.M.R. #4 foaled 1954, a Medicine Hat, with white mane and tail, shield on chest, roan markings, red roan ears, Feral Indian pony, Santo Domingo Pueblo, New Mexico. Owner: R. E. Brislawn, Oshoto, Wyoming.

I was Registrar for the first few years -.helping Bob; why the numbers like that on these horses? The plan was register the stallions first, and I did the first 7; then secondly the mares. and then their colts, but: people would buy horses from Bob, then want a low number so they could say how rare and valuable the horse was. so - Bob would say, "this horse comes first". and so from there it was first come, first serve, in an orderly fashion. The Spanish Mustang bloodlines trace back to the first horses brought to America by the Spanish Conquistadores in the early 1500s and 1600s. It was the survival of the fittest. These mustangs must not be confused with the wild horses of today as the wild horses are all of mixed breeding that have gone wild.

On the American frontier, the Spanish Mustang was Indian pony, pack horse, Cavalry mount, war horse, plow horse, cow pony, Pony Express mount, remuda horse and the horse that chased the cattle up the Texas Trail into Kansas, Nebraska, Wyoming and Montana. The Mustang is well-known for his Cow-sense and Horse-sense. He is the original horse of the Americas. He can proudly and justly claim the title, "The Horse with a Heritage". The Spanish Mustang stands 13 to 14 and 1/2 hands high and weighs between 700 and 900 pounds. He is short-coupled, and his back has only five lumbar vertebrae with only 17 ribs. The cannon bones are dense, making them extremely durable to stand up under strenuous work. The Mustang lacks feathers, except for a sparse fetlock. Chestnuts, when present, are small and smooth. Pasterns are medium long. The body is equally balanced. The distance from the poll to the withers measure the same as from the withers to the croup. The forequarters are powerful and the heart girth very deep; ot- her reasons for the Spanish Mustang's endurance. The chest is not so wide, but Vs down nicely. The hindquarters are not heavy, the croup is short, and the tail set fairly low. Two head types are found in the Spanish Mustang: coarser features, wider jowl and usually a Roman nose. The other has finer characteristics and a straight or slightly dished face. Both types have deep latches, wide-set eyes, and small well notched ears, a white sclera around the eyes is often found. These horses run the gamut of coloration including Grullos, Appaloosas, Palaminos, Blues, Overos (Medicine Hats), and shades of duns, buckskins, roans, and paints. All the common solid colors are also found. Roan hairs, mainly on the flanks and in the tail, are present in all the colors. Genes patterns, such as line-backs, Christ's Cross over the withers, and zebra stripes on the legs are common.

Bob's knowledge is from actual, "on the ground" experience and the research is not from the pages of a book, although we studied them too. We looked at paintings by the old timer artists as they had to be honest as a photograph in what they painted as anything less would be a lie. Charley Russell and Ferderic Remminton are good examples - of those times. Everything Bob said about the bones, heart, lungs, ribs, and vertebrae has been scientifically proven 100 % correct. Bob made this a non-profit organization so people couldn't say he done it/this for selfish reasons. ---Dipper

Robert Denhart

Cayuse Ranch, Oshoto, Wyoming 1969: Nejl and wife, Kitty put together the Tally Book. listing at that time the 218 horses registered in the Spanish Mustang Registry, Inc.

Among the many letters received is one from Bob Denhardt, the founder of the American Quarter Horse Registry:

Dear Bob, Nejl and Kitty UiBreaslain,

I want to congratulate you on your most excellant "Tally Book". This was real labor of love -- I know because I fought through the Vol I #I of the AQHA, (American Quarter Horse Association) and I fortunately had some millionaires helping - and they do help. I also felt a tinge when I read the "old Man's" (I'm old enough to call him that) Headaches and Hardships. I, too when I was still fighting for the old 14 hands, hard twisted, bull-dog quarter horse, whose daddy was a running horse and whose dam was a mustang; ran into the same guff from the race horse boys and the quick buck boys. Tell the "Old Man" what is to be will be,

but he did all any other four men could do - and things are not half bad.
Regards, Bob Denhardt

Topsye

Cayuse Ranch, Oshoto, Wyoming: 1959: Topsye, S.M.R.I. #34, out of Arizona Spanish Mustang stock brought to Wyoming in 1908 by the 101 Ranch, of Moorcroft, Wyoming. Topsye placed in 94 mile endurance race from Spotted Horse, Wyoming to Upton, Wyoming, time 10 hours -- 94 miles. She was 13 years old at the time. Topsye weighed 750 pounds and carried 159 pounds weight the 94 miles. She died this year 1959 at age of 27, haveing colt." ---Bob

Gusher, Utah, 1959: It was after Bob moved to Utah, that the Holbrooks, then of Fort Duchesne, Utah, registered some of their horses.

Bally, S.M.R #35, Sorrel-buckskin Mare, light mane and tail, left fore sock, right rear sock, bald face, foaled 1935. Sire: Monty (Buck). Dam: Roan Appaloosa. Owner: Sadie Holbrook.

Banjo, S.M.R. #57, Grullo Stallion, foaled 1941. Sire: Monty (Buck) and Dam: Roan Mare. Owner: Monty Holbrook.

Blondy, S.M.R. #58, Sorrel Mare, two rear stocking, right fore stocking, glass eyed, foaled 1944. Owner, Mary J. (Holbrook) Thurston.

Jack, S.M.R. #59; Light Grullo Stallion, fore socks, left

rear sock, star, foaled 1952. Sire and Dam: Feral Mustangs from Utah. ---Dipper

Section Eleven

Unexpected Danger Belts Bob Out of the Saddle

A New Horse, a New World

Oshoto, Wyoming: 1965: Well as I said before its a new world so a new horse! But where is the Horse? Ed said, they have bred all the horse out of the horse, for ribbons and show. Also, most registered horses need be softer as the novice just can't handle the old true Spanish blooded horse, like the old Steel Dust, Kentucky Whip or most any old time horse of Thoroughbred Spanish breeding.

So all was happy until an article came out in a very honest and eastern horse magazine. It all started when Governor Rockafeller signed the Bill. A public state law of New York providing funds for 4-H Club projects in 1965. Now the Board of Trustees of the fund decided to give to every 4-H Club in every county in New York State a Statue or rather a skeleton of a horse for their study. But they couldn't find a Horse or a Registered Breed with a uniform skeleton as most are Hybrid from cross and inbred breeding.

We have done a lot of research as to bones of Horses. We

had to in order to prove to the world that our horses were Puro Espanol. The true Horse had up to 6 Vertebra and 18 pair of ribs. Today we find skeletons of other horses with 7 or 8 lumbar Vertebra and 19 to 20 pair of ribs.

Maybe the truest horse today are the old time Arabs, a few left, and the Spanish Horse. And we'll have here on the Ranch the Spanish Mustang skeleton for proof.

Warren, my good friend, an Appaloosa Breeder, sent us a Rapid City, South Dakota paper as he knew we have been contacted by the Bureau of Land Management as to those feral horses in the Bryon Mountain National Wild Horse Range along the Montana-Wyoming line. The Bureau of Land Management man was here with slides of the horses and parties from Lovell, Wyoming - here with skeletons to prove these horses are not Hybred Mongrals with more than 6 large Lumbar Vertebraes or more than 18 pair ribs. And a lot carrying Spanish blood as shown by their Vertibras but they must go to give way to the modern Hybred horse. Maybe like the wonderful honest Indian, they most go. Standing in the way of progress. Now the Indian is honorated. and admired so everyone saying "I am Indian". And as Mack at the National Cowboy Hall of Fame, said "I knew him before he was an Indian".

Well, I am Irish. The Sioux were Gaelic, so I RATE. So let us save the true Horse for future generations to see.

We also checked well the feral horse of Nevada. Most are of the old Spanish cowpony strain. Spanish Morgan and Spanish Thoroughbreds, as very little draft blood in the great Southwest. As not a farming country so mostly Mules, Donkeys and Spanish cowponies.

And as ending as a Horseman of 75 years and still riding I

wish to say in favor of the feral horse - that is eating our grass - he should be saved if only for sentimental and historical reasons so the people can see the glamorous romantic horse. Maybe not quite true but at least a symbol of the Old west and the Lore of the old Mustangers. ---The Wyoming Kid

The Horses of the West

Cayuse Ranch, Oshoto, Wyoming. 1965 Being 75-years-old and knowing the West and her horses, as well as putting in thirty years as Packer, Teamster and sometimes Recorder for the Topographic Branch of the U. S. Geological Survey. Packed when parts of the Yellowstone Park was mapped and all of the Teton Park and worked in all parts of the West and Southwest, always in isolated unmapped areas.

Have met and talked with men that were born in the 1830's and 1840's. That is why I know the history of the West as to horses and Indians. So, will say, as a "Horseman", I don't mean a "Buckaroo" or "Horse trainer", but as a horseman as to our horses and as to different breeds and their ability. I will say one of the best horses today is the feral mustang; first, because he carries no Draft or Bristish Pony blood and as a whole is Kentucky Thoroughbred -- plus, Spanish.

One spot I know of where horses, mostly from Tesas, where turned out on the Salmon and Snake Rivers and as all the Southwest and most of Oregon and Idaho. Maybe 10% of the cowhorses where "Steel-Dust", "Copper Bottom" and "Kentucky Whip", breeding the 90% Spanish ponies. These Kentucky Thoroughbreds crossed on Spanish mares in Texas and were the original so-called Quarter Horses or Texas Cowhorses. Here in Wyoming and Montana they were called Texas ponies and they were ponies mostly 14 hands. Some of these Kentucky stallions were brought into Texas as early as 1845 but mostly after the Civil War.

"Well", Jones said, "By 1900 Thoroughbred stallions being shipped to Cow country and crossed on better mustang mares." So - the wild ones are the descendants of the Aristocratic Cowponies that trailed the Longhorn cattle to every part of the West.

Lets talk about "Steel-Dusts", this Legendary Kentucky Thoroughbred foaled in Kentucky in 1843 and brought to Texas in 1855. Dam unknown so definitely Spanish. Reason -- he could run, his size was 14.2 hands there is no question, but his blood added an important element to speed and stamina as well as all cowhorses and running horses of the Southwest. All the original Short Horses now are called Quarter Horses--carried more Spanish-Mustang blood than Thoroughbred blood, as one "Steel-Dust" and thousands of Spanish mares.

My son, Emmett rides "War Horse" of "Steel-Dust" blood and can run up on the wild ones. Maybe our "Yellow Fox, Registered Spanish Mustang stallion is just as fast and just because he is -- the Quarter Horse people say "Yellow Fox" is a Quarter Horse. So Emmett gets back at them by saying, "Yes, he is a Percheron".

Today, as one good Horseman said, "The horse has all been bred out of the horse by in-breeding, line-breeding and crossbreeding and as to me, three crosses is the limit as to having a good using horse. I have seen a horse with big ears, one pointing to the Jones and the other to the Smiths, you can know he is a "Dukes mixture." Horses are like a style - same as a hairdo or hat. Now the Appaloosa and Quarter Horse is in style, but there will be a new horse - a new style. The little good using Morgan went out of style and the Hamiltonian stole his thunder and took over as roads being made and easier to ride in a buggy.

The now called salesman could carry his sample cases and go to the Livery Stable in any town and get a team of Hamiltonian to go to all the better inland towns. These Hamiltonians could easily make 12 miles per hour for 3 hours. I came to Wyoming with a Hamiltonian mustang gelding. He could walk flat footed to Sundance over country-side 50 miles in less than 10 hours. We always figured to go to Sundance in 7 hours over the Bear Lodge Mountains or go to Hulett, 30 miles with little horses or light wagon in 4 hours and back the same day. These horses mostly of Mustang standard-bred blood. The little 900 to 1000 pound greyhound racing Thoroughbred are all but gone. Maybe some stables in the East still have them. Most Thoroughbred's of today are, or carry, Army Remount breeding -- "Boots and Saddle", and are refined Draft. The little old time racing Thoroughbred crossed with mustang mares gave too small a horse for the Cavalry. Your feral mustang carries the real old saddle stock blood and is the old horse the old time cowboy loved to ride. ---Bob

Landmark Meeting - at Mckinleys

September 9th and 10th, 1967; The first public meeting of the Spanish Mustang Registry was held at the McKinley ranch in New Mexico. Terry Saunders was Moderator. At this meeting they voted to not make it  a Public Organization. Rather than make it wide-open like the Quarter Horse or Appaloosas and other registries, but to keep it semi-private. ---Dipper

Another Landmark Meeting - at Ilo Belsky's

Another landmark meeting of the Spanish Mustang Registry, Inc., was held at Ilo Belsky's of Eli, Nebraska. Kent Gregerson started another registry, because we would not take the wild horses. (Kent Gregerson, National Mustang Association.) ---Dipper

Foundation Mares of the Spanish Mustang Registry

Cayuse Ranch, Oshoto, Wyoming --- September, 1967:

Cedro (left), shown at the age of 25, is a true buckskin Spanish mare. She was found by Gilbert Jones in the isolated Spanish village of Cedro, New Mexico. Cedro was the kind of mare that could head a cow, pull a plow and the kind that kept Santa Fe, El Paso and Albuquerque supplied with wood until 1920. Cedro hauled wood for her owner from above Cedro village to Albuquerque a round trip of 70 miles. They would make the trip in a day, arriving home sometime in the night.

On arriving in Albuquerque, she was turned loose in a vacant lot to graze and given two ears of corn. The Spanish man got $2.00 for his load, a little wine to go with his lunch and corn meal, coffee and sugar to take home to his family.

The Spanish people had to stop hauling wood when cars began to crowd the highways. Too many ponies and people were being killed. During 1917, I have seen the highway lined with these little ponies pulling wagons loaded with mesquite roots and pinon pine. They'd go down the road with wheel hubs smoking since the only wagon grease in those days was wool fat.

Cedro died in Oklahoma at the age of 30. She left us several nice duns and buckskins.

Queenie, (center), a Medicine Hat overo paint, was brought from the Crow Reservation in Montana in 1925 by Charles and Dick Williams. Queenie had blue roan markings and bonnet and glass eyes. She stood under 14 hands and weighed 850 pounds. She was a fast running mare and a good cow pony. At 28 years, she had a stroke, fell to her knees, her legs paralyzed, and was unable to get up. We fed her on the ground and watered her through a tube for twenty-eight days before she finally died. So rugged a mare, it took her nearly a month for her to die!

Teton (right), was a purple roan Shoshoni mare. Age 24. She had all the characteristics and markings of most Indian Mustangs: vertical striped hooves, white sclera around the eyes, and a paper or big blazed face. She stood 13.3 and weighed 800 pounds. Her skin was dark, not the mottled pink of most Medicine Hats and white horses. Notice how her front legs V-up, showing a narrow but deep chest.

Teton was found by Larry Richards in a pack string in the Tetons of Wyoming. I have ridden this mare through prairie dog towns chasing range horses and she'd dodge the holes so fast you'd have to grab the horn. Teton died at age 32 in Oklahoma, after getting in a bog hole. She had a four-month old filly by her side at the time.

The buckskin mare, Mexicali Rose, came out of northern Mexico near what is known as the "jog." She had no brand, just the slit ear used by an outlaw gang that operated in the area. This gang raided across the border into Mexico, bringing out anything from a pig, to horses and cattle. Mexi died in the big blizzard that hit Wyoming last May. All her colts have been exceptionally nice Spanish ponies. ---R. E. Brislawn

The Glory Past and the Troubles Ahead

Bob wrote to tell me that those two little Spanish Mustangs were in a small pen as in a jail cell, or zoo cage, for people to walk by and look at, but no room to run and rump so unlike their many hills of home. We don't know what happened to these horses after Bob was kicked out of the National Cowboy Hall of Fame...at Oklahoma City, Oklahoma, but they were gotten rid of - somehow, somewhere......

There were others people in the registry who were not always for the purity, and were for only one type of horse instead of all five types that had evolved by the law of the wild, the survival of the fittest, in different areas of the United States.

Some even went so far as to try to change the name of the Spanish Mustang Registry, Incorporated, to Spanish Barb Mustang Registry, with just the Barb Type.

There were others who wanted to bring in the British Pony blood for the fancy show coloration, and those who said the Tobiano color was Spanish, they just didn't give a darn or else hadn't dug through the half-rotted carcasses of recently dead horses to study their Vertebras and bones; Or the old dried bones of the long-time dead. ---Dipper

Let Us Face It

Cayuse Ranch, Oshoto, Wyoming February 27, 1969:

What is the fight over? Why not lay the cards on the table, and come out in the open, like a brave man?

Now after twelve years of search, study, and research we have them straight. So a new set up, to change the name, but it is the same old registry and will be based on purity and a new brochure to prove this; with pictures of the horses and their vertebra as proof. Then and not until then will we be recognized by the public. A registry based on purity, and honesty but not a farce. About the National Cowboy Hall of Fame, they are already there. Is there a question as to them? If so step forth and say it!!!! Is there anything wrong with the purity except the size? We didn't spend three small fortunes, time and hardships to bring them back impure!!!!

If all goes as plans there will be a reserve for two stud bunches and this reserve willed to the Spanish Mustang. This to me is much safer then the Hall of Fame as there will be no arguments as to what stallions or mares, that from time to time will be alternated. All registered horses now in will automatically come in as definitely no split registry. It is still the same old registry. ---Bob

P. S. If and when the private reserve, name maybe Trueblood Ranch or Broomtail Ranch. ---Bob

Note: Bob did make this reserve for the Spanish Mustangs

and named it The Trueblood Reserve.

On Changing the Name of the Registry

The Directors, of the Spanish Mustang Registry, Incorporated, held a vote by mail. I have the postcard Bob received from the Emminent Lawrence P. Richards:

"April 2, 1969 11:30 P.M. Dear Friend, Bob, and Family:

It surely was great to talk to you on the phone tonight. It took me right back to 1955, when we first visited you. You sounded JUST THE SAME, I could SMELL the sagebrush; and I could hear (in my mind) the thunder, the pouring rain, and the big hail stones falling. (Do you remember? You said, "I had brought the rain, and that was good luck", and that I must be part Irish, which I am -- about 20% to 25%, I guess.)

Yes, I am in favor of keeping the name of our registry the same: The Spanish Mustang Registry, Inc. I'm proud of it! It has stood for 12 years. It might cause a lot of humbug to change it on all the registration papers, etc., and, as you pointed out, a change might bring us a complicated law-suit. Please tell Richard Macy that I an NOT in favor of changing the name.

My apologies for not answering your good letters & Christmas Card. We will be out to see you in Oshoto this summer. Please send me another sprig of sagebrush as you did when I was in New Guinea." --Signed "Larry"

It was voted not to change the name, and so it remains The

Spanish Mustang Registry, Incorporated. ---Dipper

Oshoto, Wyoming June 28, 1969:

Bob Voted Out Director's Meeting

Brislawn Cayuse Ranch, Oshoto, Wyoming, July 11, 1969;

A `Directors' Meeting of the Spanish Mustang Registry was held. The Minutes to this meeting are as follows:

Members Present: Robert E. Brislawn, Sr., President: Robert E. Brislawn, Jr. Vice-President; Lawrence P. Richards, Ph.D, a Director; and Mrs. Gioja Brislawn, a member and observer. The meeting was called to order by Bob Brislawn at 7:30 A.M.

It was here that Bob was asked to resign as President and as a Director because of his health as it was humanly impossible for one person to do everything and for the best interests of the organization, so the business could be run more efficiently and effectively. It was one of the hardest things for them to do but it freed up Bob to go on to work in other areas of the horse world that needed his guidance. Bob remained as a voting member and as "Founding Father" of the Spanish Mustang Registry, Inc. Bob accepted gladly.

It was proposed by Larry Richards and unanimously agreed that Ferdy Brislawn also be designated (if he so wishes) a "Founding Father" of our Registry.

It was proposed by Bob Brislawn and agreed by Larry

Richards and Bob that Emmett Brislawn be recognized by the Registry as one of the most important contributors (1) to the continuation of the work of perpetuating the ideals of the Registry and the purity of the mustangs originally collected by his father, his uncle, and by other persons, and (2) to the capturing in the wild or collection and preservation of the mustangs and/or mustang-type horses of equal degree of authenticity and value (as the original foundation animals) to our Registry.

It was proposed by Bob Brislawn and Larry Richards and unanimously agreed that R. Emmett Brislawn, Jr., be designated President of the Spanish Mustang Registry.

It was proposed by Larry Richards and unanimously agreed that Bob Racicot be designated as a Director.

It was proposed by Larry Richards and unanimously agreed that the Directors accept the written resignation from the office of Registrar of Neil UiBreaslain (See letter of June 15, 1969, from Neil Brislawn to Bob Racicot. Neil said that he would not continue with out his Dad.)

It was proposed by Larry Richards and unanimously agreed that the President, Directors, and all interested members meet on August 13-14, 1969 at Hamilton, Montana. To continue the original and fundamental work of our Registry and to endeavor to establish more efficient and effective methods of carrying out this work.

It was proposed by Bob Brislawn and unanimously agreed that we endeavor to prove the basic excellent qualities and abilities of our registered mustangs in the areas of cattle cutting, calf roping, endurance riding, trail riding, barrel racing, trick riding, jumping, pleasure riding, gymkhana, conformation showing, or any other legitimate form of horsemanship or horse showmanship for the purpose of honestly promoting them to other interested horsemen as excellent all-around using horses and as horses of great rarity and historical importence and romance in the heritage of our nation.

The meeting was adjourned at 8 A.M. Respectfully submitted to the Members of our Registry (and signed) by: Robert E. Brialwn, Sr., past President and Founding Father, Emmett Brislawn, (new) President, Lawrence P. Richards, Ph.D, Director (and acting Secretary), and Gioja Brislawn, Member and observer.

If a Man Knew His Way Around

When we formed the Spanish Mustang Registry, Inc., the Brislawn's and the Eminent Lawrence P. Richards, Ph.D., Dr. Richards and Bob Brislawn had contacted everyone from Bob Denhardt and Wayne Densmore, to J. Frank Dobie.

J. Frank Dobie said "he was very sorry, he could only give his moral support because the man that wrote THE MUSTANGS had it all taken out of him physically". But he went on to state in his letter to Dr. Richards, "that he felt very certain that the Spanish Horse could be restored if a man knew his way around".

We (Brislawns) start out to see what we could do, and after

175

twelve years of study, hardships, and fortunes spent, we now have eleven little mares and two little studs to be put on a reserve, that we feel are as pure as the day they landed in North America. Proof of their authenticity is their skeletons, hair, chestnuts, ergots, fetlocks, primitive conformation such as low set tails, deep narrow chests that `V' up nicely (front legs close set together).

We have a reserve of eight hundred acres on the Lone Star Texas Trail in the Red Fox Hills, to be willed to the Mustang of the Indian, the Horse of the Spaniards. As to the name of the reserve, we are glad to have suggestions. We are starting with "True Blood Reserve" as a tentative name.

This project will undoubtedly need moral and financial, may be sometimes physical, support. The layman are behind us. I stand on purity the spinal columns of the Mustang of the Indian, Horse of the Spaniard. Do You????? ---Bob

(signed:) R. E. Brislawn, Nejl and Kitty UiBreaslain

--- end volume one ---

Misery loved your company ...

Made in United States
Troutdale, OR
09/24/2023

13155640R00106